POESIS

flowing along a river of time

POESIS
flowing along a river of time

AARON WILLIAM PERRY

with illustrations by
Indigo Hunter Chesnutt-Perry

EARTH WATER PRESS
amplifying voices for the world

Copyright © 2020 Aaron William Perry

Poesis – Flowing Along a River of Time

ISBN: 978-1-7347229-2-5 (hardcover)
ISBN: 978-1-7347229-1-8 (paperback)
ISBN: 978-1-7347229-3-2 (ebook)

All rights reserved. No part of this book may be reproduced in any form or by any electronic or mechanical means, including information storage and retrieval systems, without permission in writing from the publisher, except by reviewers, who may quote brief passages in a review.

Library of Congress Control Number: 2020940090

Illustrations: Indigo Hunter Chesnutt-Perry
Cover Design: Jake Welsh
Book Design: Maggie McLaughlin

Earth Water Press
Denver Colorado
www.earthwaterpress.com

Printed in the United States of America

Contents

Introduction	xiii
1. Cotton-Wooded Buddhas	1
2. Along Water's Edge	2
3. Azure-Eyed Songbird (for Amanda)	3
4. Beat City Lights	5
5. Bathroom Stall (Game #1)	7
6. Gurgling Swirling Flow (Game #2)	8
7. Journey & Homeward Return	9
8. Leaving Corsica	10
9. Like the Arctic Tern, We Are	11
10. Moon-Night, Anasazi Dream Song	12
11. Paris, Mid-Day Autumn	14
12. Soon Dawn – (Desert Death)	15
13. Soul's Memories	17
14. 'Tis Autumn	18
15. Universe (University)	19
16. Washington Square, Autumn	20
17. Winter, We	21
18. Without Death, All Is Meaningless	22
19. Boulder Haze Evening	23
20. Cosmos / Truth	25
21. Consider Yourself Human	27
22. Everything Pulsing	29
23. Old Frontiers (for my Father)	30
24. Snow Falls Down	31
25. Strange the Marriage	33
26. Sun Down Now	34
27. From Modern Hands	35
28. Gnarled Spruce Blues	37
29. Mist Droplet	39
30. Tired Branches	40
31. We Gather	42

32.	We March Quietly	43
33.	We Soon Recrudesce	45
34.	We're From Kuchu Sharvi	46
35.	Wretched	48
36.	Sunshine Gushing Up	49
37.	Ecocapricitopic	51
38.	Biotopic Villages	53
39.	Come Down Rivers	54
40.	Brick Path	55
41.	Cooperative Narcissism (At a Poetry Reading)	56
42.	In Durango Pub	58
43.	Tranquil Night	59
44.	We Mist Children	61
45.	Mind Junkies Need Gaia Cure	62
46.	Oh World!	63
47.	I Must Just Listen	64
48.	Seven Fathers	65
49.	Synchronistic Encounter	66
50.	Behind Horizon	67
51.	Healing Waters	69
52.	An Evening of Big Medicine	70
53.	Poetic Winds Gathering	71
54.	Wet Moon	73
55.	Fire Keeper	74
56.	Soft Kiss of Winter	76
57.	Ad Lucem – A Degree of Initiation	77
58.	I was once there…	78
59.	Milestones in the River of Time	81
60.	Rafael's Song in Seattle's Waters	83
61.	There Is A Center	84
62.	What If You Knew?	85
63.	As Our Paths Diverge	87
64.	Grandpa Bear Passing	88
65.	Trusting Divine Wind	90
66.	I Am Connected to Divine Feminine	91

67. A Westward Quest – A Rite of Initiation	93
68. Our Brothers & Sisters Gather	96
69. Unresolved Stanzas (Incomplete)	100
70. Who am I? – Weird Grace Flows All Around	103
71. To the Women I (Have) Love(ed)	104
72. Shooting Stars Sailing at their Apogees –or– The Cabin of Our Awakening	105
73. Poesis – A Man's Love of Writing	111
74. New Stones Quarried	114
75. Wisdom Precipitating Into Our Bodies	117
76. We Are Creators	119
77. Time – 'Tis Cliché to Ponder Your Vagaries	120
78. Alesia Алеся	122
79. Honey & Two Red Roses at the Pillared Gate	124
80. Do You Feel It?	126
81. 1000 Dreams Forever (For Nicolette)	127
82. Where Are You Hiding?	129
83. We'll All Be Dead Soon	131
84. What If…	133
Acknowledgements	135
A Note on the Locations	137
About the Poet and the Artist	141

Range after range of mountains.
Year after year after year.
I am still in love.

—GARY SNYDER

It is easier to build strong children than to
repair broken men

—FREDERICK DOUGLASS

If you can dream – and not make dreams your master;
If you can think – and not make thoughts your aim;
If you can meet with Triumph and Disaster
And treat those two impostors just the same…
If you can talk with crowds and keep your virtue,
Or walk with Kings – nor lose the common touch…
you'll be a Man, my son!

—RUDYARD KIPLING, "If"

For my children

Introduction

I am thrilled to share this collection of poetry with you. It follows the arc of my adulthood thus far, which I optimistically refer to as "the early years." Sharing these poems with you is a peculiar and vulnerable thing to do. I am letting you in on some of my most intimate, most cherished, and most revealing moments. You'll find an unusually animated and deep-seeded connection with the natural living world—something that has been my "normal" since my earliest childhood. You'll find romantic love, longing, and the heart ache that can accompany this most complex type of human connection. You'll find a wildly Dionysian passion for life, and, later, the more "sober" expressions of a man who has struggled with alcoholism. Through it all, I hope you will find threads of empowerment, purpose, and inspiration from my life-long commitment to stewardship, regeneration and healing our Mother Earth, and our cultural, social, and personal pathologies.

In this arc you'll find pain, joy, ecstasy, tumult, intimacy; love, loss, and the profound experience of having two remarkable children—my daughter Osha Asa and my son Indigo Hunter—at a young age. As I pen this introduction in my early forties, my daughter is finishing up her undergraduate studies in neuro science, and preparing to take the MCAT entrance exams for medical school. My son is graduating high school in the time of the Corona Virus—making it a strangely anticlimactic conclusion to his childhood years, but an extraordinary context for that momentous milestone he'll forever share with his contemporaries. He is preparing to study architecture, and looking forward to returning to the Rocky Mountain West after a long and formative sojourn in St. Louis.

Although a writer, I cannot easily express with words how proud I am of my two children, and, moreover, how profoundly grateful I am to have them as friends, colleagues, and companions in this strange, miraculous adventure called life. My daughter is now older than her mother Amanda and I were

when we had her. My son is now about the same age I was when I penned "Cotton Wooded Buddhas" —the first poem in this collection. That is a strange thing to ponder. Life truly is a river of time, and time seems to bend and fold upon itself as we go through it. In my experience, parenthood has a way of augmenting and revealing this strange phenomenon like nothing else.

This publication is an especially meaningful one to me, as it is a collaboration with my dear boy Hunter. Although he's very much a man now, towering over me at 6'4", and faster, stronger and defter on the basketball court and in the gym, he will always be my "boy." His beautiful, meticulous, and mysterious artwork is a tremendous accompaniment to the poetry—some of which celebrates our path together as father and son. The poem "Fire Keeper" was written for Hunter's 13th birthday, and was presented to him, along with letters from Amanda, Osha, and his extended family, on the evening of his first solo camping in the wilderness—a rite of passage. This was in a very special area in the Indian Peaks Wilderness outside of Nederland, Colorado—not far from where parts of his and his sister's placentas were buried after their births, and quite possibly where he was in fact conceived. That is what being connected to place looks and feels like—something our ancestors felt and knew way more deeply than most of us today, for now at least. The poem "A Westward Quest—A Rite of Initiation" commemorates an epic journey That Hunter and I took for his 16th birthday—driving from Colorado through Utah and Nevada to California and back. We visited sacred sites, we shared ceremony, we listened to all kinds of music—from rap to down tempo to classical. We chilled in the wilderness with desert solitude, towering Sitka Spruce trees, and ocean vistas, and we hung out at Venice Beach—where Hunter schooled some very serious basketball players in his quiet, humble, powerful warrior way.

Poesis – flowing along a river of time

To be able to share all of this with you is above all else an expression of love for my children. To send these celebratory ripples into the cosmic fabric by sharing these poems with you is a song and prayer of love and gratitude.

May all of this touch your heart as well.

In this strange time of the Corona Virus, it has been a strangely surreal experience to record videos of myself reading many of these poems and sharing them through social media. As challenging as these times are, and as much suffering as they are causing, they are also a gift of awakening, of slowing down, and of reconnecting in a humble, rooted manner to the soil, to our environs, to cooking and baking, to playing games with family, and to listening to the somehow brighter and more enthusiastic bird song that surrounds us. This may well be the miraculous doorway opening up that will allow our peculiar adolescent species to enter into a more mature adulthood—one in which we're actually capable of fulfilling our deepest purpose and obligation to take good great care of this beautiful creation, and of each other. May we each discover and cultivate a deepening connection with *Oikos*, with *Veriditas*, with *Light*, and with the elemental admixture of life from death we call *Soil*. May we heal, grow, and come to see the reality of this miraculous living planet Earth with clear eyes, deep gratitude, and humble joy.

May we learn to truly *Love*. May it be so.

Aaron William Perry
Boulder, Colorado
May 2020

Cotton-Wooded Buddhas
Denver, CO – 1996

Thoughts perched on fallen
Willow ... nothingness carried
off by faint breeze of dusk.
Towering around me are
the silent, still Buddhas...
Now gray, solemn, speaking
Steadily of nothing, and
I listen attentively. Flesh
Becoming fallen willow as
Spirit floats around in
The never-ness of now...

Sun setting on today, reeds
Click-clacking in their patient
Koan-dance, fires blazing
now in the last farewell
embrace before nightfall.

The cloud-fire slowly
burns itself out again.
Tangerine-pink vessels sail
on in ever darkening
seasky.

Cotton-Wooded Buddhas
keep on singing their gold-song.
Swirling, sinking into the
Night, I wander back
through the rushes, taking
My time in forever wonder.

Along Water's Edge
New York, NY – 1996

Along water's edge
We roost, noisy squalor
Speak of supposed quiet.

But it's not silence.

Greyed, aged squawkers
Speak to yearlings, describe
Roost, roosting.

Lined 'knowledge' presses on.

'Out there deep sea looms'
Young, convinced not to go
Must roost, roosting.

We peer out to dark sea.

Along shallow, lined shoal.

Shallow, lined shoal
Appears deep, complex
So we're told.

Waves swirl, tides rise, fall.

'And did you see all the nuance?'
Greyed foul questions young

But we're undistracted now.

Heads turned seaward,
Grey squawks fade.
Flight enticed, we peer beyond.

Wings shake
Deep sea – out there
Calls.

Silence.

WE listen. New teachers

Soon fly. Soon fly.
Peer.
Listen.

Fly.

Azure-Eyed Songbird (for Amanda)
Corsica, France – 1996

Azure-eyed songbird:
Climbs, sails, teases mountain-breeze.
Carefree in fresh daylight, tender,
Flighty being caresses the world's winds.

I nearby sit and watch meadow lark
Fluttering about, singing sweet morning-hymns.
And tiny dulce-voice sends minuets floating
On the lazy breeze: far flung breath feathers.

Absorbed in golden silk sun-flight,
Soft tears streak apricot cheeks.
Forever between open meadow, dark oak;
Gloomy deep leaf-shade and bright field glee.

Near stream, winged lady alights, sorrowful, quiet.
I cajole a smile… in vain.
Un-sure feet slip on mossed water-rocks:
She plunges into babbling wetness, unmoving granite.

I approach, uncertain, abashed…
Soaked, bruised, vague eyes turn, peer, draw near.
I laugh, for she's stunned but smiling:
Once again, dark oak's momentarily felled, and

Embraced in tears, in laughter
We assure ourselves that love doth live…
Carefree in fresh daylight, tender,
Flighty being caresses world's winds.

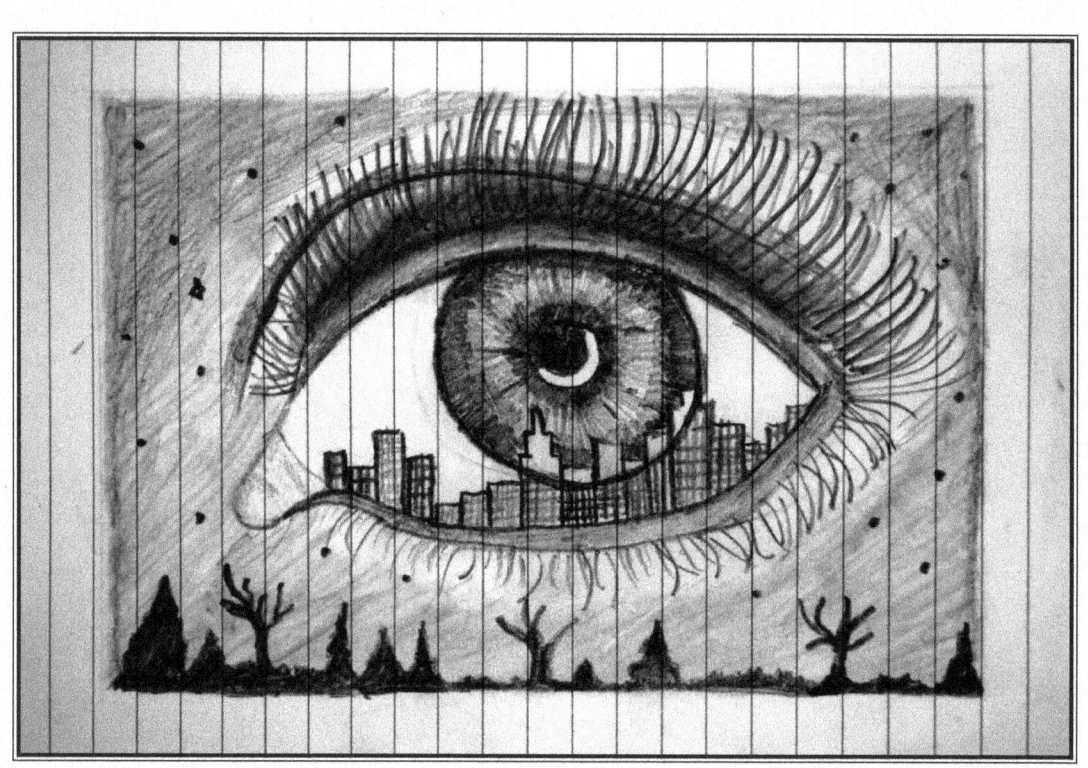

Beat City Lights
New York, NY & Boulder, CO – 1996

beat city lights bopped
all around cool minds
junked eyes wide
lusting in midnight
   insanity

everywhere tappity taps –
faucet drops (eternal
   chromed mantra)
snared rhythms
scribbling pen dances
skippity skops

late western nights in
   midsummer
east village
   congregations of not
   so holy saints
miles and miles of tones
colors swirling mosaics

coal trains rumble by
   – OM
and some hop on
bummed dharmas
   eulogize
soon enveloping brahma
and some blow wildly

out west brassed
   proclamations of BE
japhy's mountainside
   howls
mingle with unstill
   winds
eventual breath of
   manhattan
lungs gasping – roaring

lucky strike smoke
   lingers
with stacked smog
   makers
and move on swirl move
   on

sweet trill up pentatonic
   exclamation
nothing but blue... all
   blues
in land of intoxication
all moving long some
   road
on some road to
   somewhere

why remain silent

cacophonous march into
   approaching
abyss
it is beautiful

slip into deep warm
   wake sleep dens
of mindlessness
bohemian buddhas
wander – up fretless
   bass right
low growls moans holds
   together
keeps some time,
   anytime
which is off most of the
   time anyway
or may as well be

when its right up –

back down to lodo
and urban stars
twinkle and guide
the absurd voyage
   onward

to somewhere
anywhere
nowhere

why not make some
   noise
gag a do gada do wop
ourselves through
   stormy
nights and whose
   straight
nope... chase her
chase her forever

blow blow equinox odes
to thousand night eyes
junked and sleepy but
   awake
somehow

cool out west cool
and hot and lusty
storms forever ragin'
inside virtuous minds

tempests bigger than
   selves
explode for later
selves to temper
some later tempus
   fugit
just flies
                 >>>

into purple nightscapes
of something
strangers confuse to
   create
the strange
which is us
in a song
in a poem
in a mind – a strange
path to mindlessness

numbered expressions
   of be
so it's called bop

out west desert nights
and m.c. blues of some
   sort
perfect synthesis in
   moment
of three four straight
   ahead
walking… in some
   minds

or in some feet too
probably fretless, usually,
   sometimes

jazz beats on

beats jazz on

and in some sticky song
bind us to now
for now
maybe

cool minds see
as beat city lights
   bopped
post modern birthing of
post post modern
   birthing
of insanity

and living within sanity
is as crazy as ever never
always
jacked john miles in
   allen alleys

birth us now

cool

is born
and bastard minds
confuse confusingness
with being

be

what's the difference
its jazz to me
beat beat beat

what a night!
what?
nothing.
oh…
thanks…
it's nothing.
oh…
what?

Bathroom Stall (Game #1)
New York, NY – 1996

bathroom stall
no door

shit
and some written on the walls,

well,
three of them.

but the fourth:
no shit

door

Gurgling Swirling Flow (Game #2)
New York, NY – 1996

    gurgling swirling flow
                                    flow
                                            flow

    passes by: verdant
        also grey   also grey
    flow river around
           swirling
                 in me

Journey & Homeward Return
Paris, France – 1996

I love the journey
Sweetened by its homeward return…

And I adore the oikos-hearth
From which I may once again venture.

Leaving Corsica
Corsica, France – 1996

Heavy clouds… grey, thick.
Splashed golden over western mountains
Steady rumble of Danielle Casanova:
Marsaille-bound "Ferryteranée."

Concrete straight-lined shore
The modern wharf – as anywhere else, now.
And city lights, urban stars begin to twinkle.
It's dusk, and night swiftly comes to Bastia.

Boy, young, passes by with too long fishing poles…
I smile, he returns… happiness radiates between
And I wonder if in his satchel he treasures caught fishes.
But I don't know how to ask: "Tu a pesce oujourdhuis?"

Two baguettes and a bag of apples…
Our dinner, our breakfast, c'est bon!
After three weeks in Corse paradise, the Garden,
We're off, and Venzolasca quickly fades to memory.

And so I smoke, and so I write…
For we travel so'more tonight.
Hand casting anti-peach light on paper
As ink falls to tell a tale… to tell a tale.

Of Corse I now know something…
Of course I'm knowing nothing
But the night swiftly comes,
And of human celeste I paint, I write.

Like the Arctic Tern, We Are
Corsica, France – 1996

Like the Arctic Tern, we are...
Flying from frozen bound to bound.
Humanity ebbs and flows forever
Between Nord and Sud Ice-Gods.

Upon inferno desert sands we've progressed
In an ageless twilight of poesis-singing
Deep purple cosmos envelopes our beings
As we praise and dread the fleeting Sun.

So some have from solid Earth
Sliced and carved great pyramids, menacing obelisks.
In vain Babel-building –
And ceased, forgotten to sing... to Be.

In not-so-distant past,
Our ancestors fled the parched dust
Of true Eden wandering – topos
And on papyrus began to clip winged songs.

We're left with confused knowledge –
Closed eyes, deaf ears have scribbled
Countless words in lifeless volumes
That scholars spoon into our hungry minds.

So we've settled, no longer flying, no longer singing
And strike out blindly – something lacks...
In our mega-polises we search vainly,
While the Evasive persists forever in Great Desert.

Some may return, may strap to tender feet
Dusted sandals of Tao – take up flutes
And satchels, Fire and staves and
Begin to sing anew the Creation Songs.

Perhaps we ought travel out our walls – now
Elusive, now almost ubiquitous – and even with
Help from Mescalito, laugh as cities crumble
In our minds – and we relearn to sing the Dreamtime.

Moon-Night, Anasazi Dream Song
Corsica, France (re: Canyonlands) – 1996

Golden moth-dust specks fly at us
From twilighted (twilit) desert horizon.

Dancing around fire-fueled by deep-canyon essence, –
WE fly, naked to the zenithed moonlight.

Unfathomable purple cosmos cradles us:
Feathers hovering, fluttering on nocturnal canyon rim.

Unwet spray drifts up from chasm-ocean filled phosphorescence –
And I follow sweet wind-water to cliff's-edge.

Below, in reflexed celestial-mare, luminous dolphins
Circle and sing silent songs – Creation... Poetry.

Mescalito guides us, seven dancers, even though we've
No button found – only inhaled verdant clouds – Euphoria.

And all around echo eternal songs of the Ancient Ones –
As we, in Dreamtime fantasm-scape, sing anew the World.

In Harmony, breaths of all the Luminous Beings meld,
And we are reborn, waking to traverse the sun-parched desert.

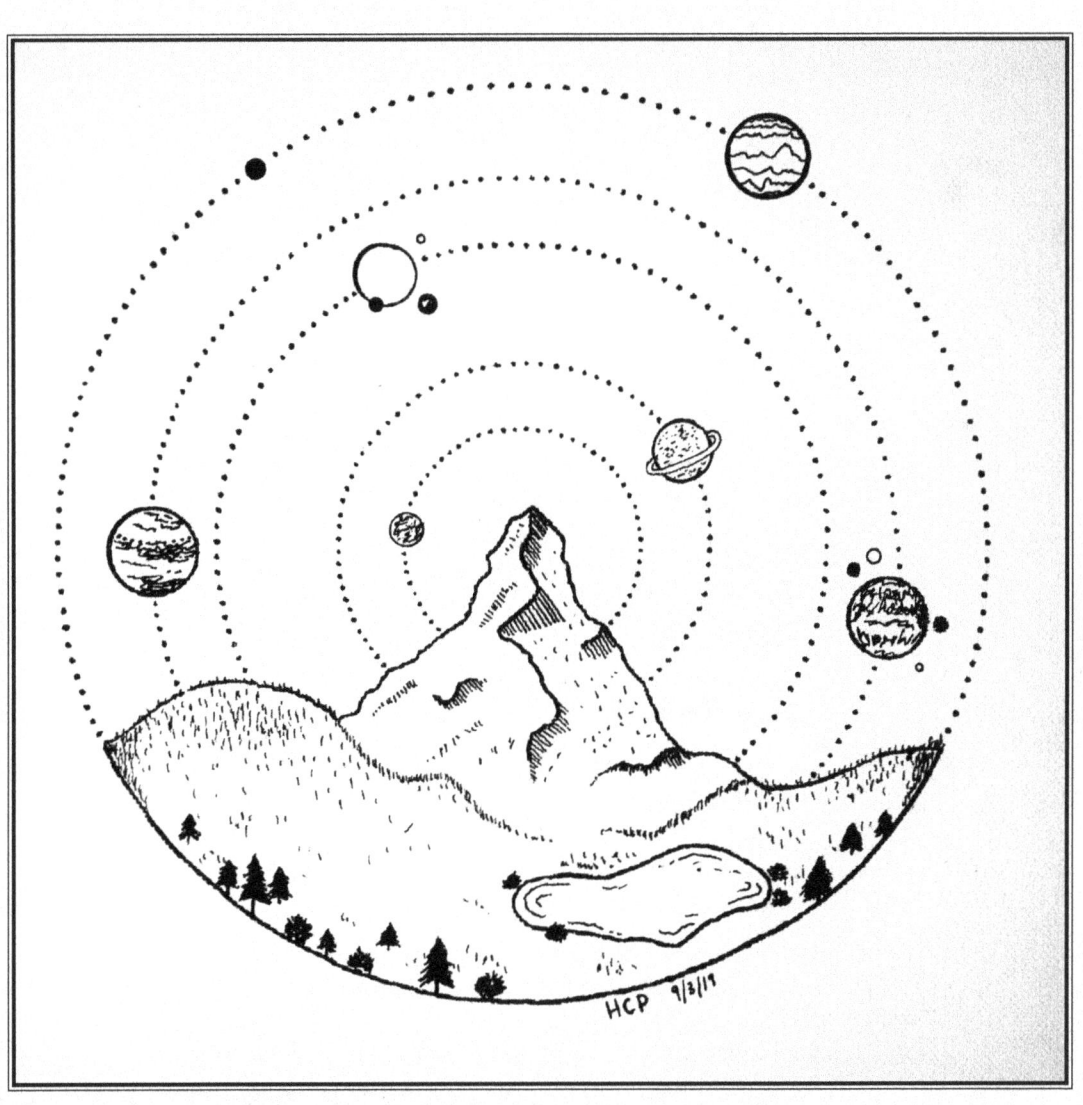

Paris, Mid-Day Autumn
Paris, France – 1996

What'd you know?...
Back in Paris.
Swift whisk *en train* from Marsailles –
Of course, back at ol' Shakespeare's...

And old man Whitman
Stares me down with glaring eyes –
Suppose I'm soiling his "news" –
Must rummage through the "oldes"...

He's a bit senile anyway – neo-expatriate
Giles reassures and we meet.
He's sickened by the bullshit –
Been Austin, Seattle, West.

I wonder how Paris stands as remedy?
But it's for a while he's here...
A brief sojourn 'for getting sick again
And perhaps he's just feeling the primal pull.

Wanderin', wonderin', wanderin'
From desert dust,
Through urban muck, ailing
Return to brief desert dusk and be.
Return to eternal desert dusk and become!

So my soul's now marked. Historied
With Paris, with ex-patriotism sympathie
But I soon return to a known place...
I soon walk alone or companioned in the desert
I continue to wander, persisting in wonder.

Soon Dawn – (Desert Death)
Corsica, France (re: Canyonlands) – 1996

Enveloped in cosmos: deep deep purple, everywhere stars
   Feint red-rimmed horizon – canyon abyss of midnight sea blue-black
      And flowing, flowing, flowing …
         On cliff's edge I sit, and with aged, worn hands,
            Gently caress Eagle's feather, found somewhere, everywhere
               I sit. I sing being songs. I become the night. I die.
                  Unwarm, uncold, desert … Unmoving, unstill celest …
                     Silent, audible, wind … wanders on, wanders on.
                        And now all's dark, all's still, all's hushed in anticipation –
                           East-horizon glow's barely felt …
                              We sense it, luminous bodies sense
                                 The return of the Golden Warrior.
                                    But I've desert dust become, and
                                        Forever laughing, am in ochre-grained
                                            Perfection: sky-pallet
                                               Endless, endless desert dust:
                                                   Golden moth specks,
                                                       Always hovering, always floating.

Soul's Memories
Corsica, France – 1996

Back down from Jossen paradise…
Descending the depths of my soul's memories.
And along curved Corse asphalt, stringing these
Mountain village beads into an ancient, priceless
Necklace, I'm singing with rhythmed steps my internal dialogue.

Consumes me… beholds me, and like sporadic autos
Whizzing by, I glimpse fleeing facades of the unfathomable,
Rotating crystal de illumination… memories, if you like.
And I was once a firefighter… childhood nagual traveling
Has left fossilized curiosities on my aging tonal… and I search.

Down old Corsican wind-snake, black thread
And deep lived mosaic spins before my mind's eye…
We walk on, we walk on, and gurgling by,
Afternoon brook song melds with sparrow accompaniment
And in silence I sing… in silence I sing!

'Tis Autumn
Corsica, France – 1996

Fire!   Fire!   Fire!
In cool blaze the oak transcends
Treedom… 'tis autumn!

Universe (University)
New York, NY – 1996

And so to white-pillar'd slaughter I drag my bleating Self.
Before me They've done the same;
Desert travelers,
Named.
Mark'd urban Cain bellows in convoluted madness.
Shuttering soul peers west.
Moist eyes long,
Obsidian.

Unmoved, I pull terror-silenced Self ever close.
Thick wine curls 'round trembling pedes.
Unsheathed saber gleams,
Blood.

Self, frozen, I hoist to marbled block, submissed.
Warm crimson flies, another death.
This one I hope's
Accept'd.

Into chasm-eyes I gaze, still, glassed.
Upon seeing, shutter.
Notice I was
Abel.

Washington Square, Autumn
New York, NY – 1996

Out here...
Cold.
Free.
Winter sets in
Iron hibernation,
But no rest.

Out here...
Evening
Gold settles,
Paints park
Subdued hue,
But no silence.

Out here...

                Standing on vortex
                Cliff's Edge
                Moment

                              standing on vortex
                                  cliff's edge
                                    moment

STANDING
ON   VORTEX
CLIFFS.
EDGE.

MOMENT.

Winter, We
New York, NY – 1996

Autumn mist down.
Heavy Heavens on
Greyed city land.

They're from afar, they're from afar: wind flung current feathers.

Iron teeth tear
Slowly shred, devour
Floating feather bed.

Caelum-clay accepts, slowly sails: but blocked, so blocked.

Blazing leaves down.
On green, cool
Fire rages, futile.

Death, decay, this crimson painted gold cannot devour.

But soon winter.
White-robed Death
Leers behind dumb cotton.

Diverse, ubiquitous splendor, Ra-endowed glory.

Absurd. We.
Defiant, compost –
Dreading, blaze.

'Neath white blanket, we won't lie down, won't suffocate.

Nothing remains.
Sun-splashed song,
Only soul breath remains.

Silence.   Death.   Soon Winter.

Without Death, All Is Meaningless
Corsica, France – 1996

Without Death, all is meaningless;
Absurd, absurd, absurd.
Crystalline Truth melts away to
Black, endless Nothing-water.
No light without death, no Light.

Ah, but we are luminous beings –
Phosphorescent threads spun in
Unfathomable, stupendous light-web.
Yes, Seattle knew, spoke, we listened:
'Life of Web,' we aren't weavers, but threads!

Oval-esque, we've two centers to our beings.
An apparently impossible paradox…
But we've a glimmer of why They speak apophatically!
Both Reason and Will make our interior,
But, unharmonized, we aimlessly in dust confuse.

We have to believe, the Warrior this knows…
This is the TAO, this is the <u>only</u> way.
Over left shoulder lurks our Death, our connection,
Our meaning, our escape from otherwise baffling Absurdity.

We must know our death, we must trust the dusked desert horizon.

Boulder Haze Evening
Boulder, CO – 1997

Boulder haze evening

Niwot's river flows on
    and on
    and on

I walk   then pause

    think
    write
    think

Logos grip temporarily holds
But I soon free
And walk
Again

Pissed parents consider me lost
insane, addicted
But this is
Not so,
Really!

Profess sanity now,
And you're just
Blind to the
Real situation

But that's okay...its
ALL   ABSURD
anyway

I just wish my folks'd
Love and Appreciate
my   self

maybe someday,   maybe someday

    maybe

    maybe

    not

Poesis – flowing along a river of time

Cosmos / Truth
Early Winter, Boulder, CO – 1997

...

...

*Poetry is an echo,
asking a shadow to dance.*

—CARL SANDBURG

Consider Yourself Human
Colorado – 200x

Consider yourself human
Not mere politician...
Speaker for politica.
Nor mere artist...
Creator and seer of beauty
Nor farmer...
Tiller and keeper of soils.

All of these, rather,
And more...
So much more!

Consider yourself human!
Father and mystic!
Mother and poet!
Child and conductor of
Life's business!

Consider yourself human!

Everything Pulsing
Little Falls, NY – 1997

pulsing everything pulsing
or oscillating
flowing, back forthing
cycling

or circle

to the mystics, the poets,
the natives and nomads
the seers, the grounded
the walkers, travelers
adventurers, people

of the Earth

rising ebbing peoples
melding moving flowing
rivers, winds
mountains even

Earth

frozen lake glass
that burps and gurgles
moans and cries
to us listeners
Earth
season progressions
reminding us of

Earth

of ourselves
Brahma, God, YHWH, Gaia, Corn Woman, Buddha,
 Sophia, Christos, White Buffalo Calf Woman
soothes and is
pulsing
everything
pulsing

Earth

Old Frontiers (for my Father)
Little Falls, NY – Christmas 1997

old frontiers
now passed over.
left behind.
memories.
so we eastward
return
and walk, pining.
great grandpa's lands
to me.
or grandpa's lands
to him.
father
and I
stroll, chat, smoke.
he visits aged
farm land splendor…
peaceful flowing stream
and speaks.
words float, hover
on still winter air
meld with my mind
to imagine
my self
before I knew
my self
somehow
barn burnt years ago
tragic pyre

ashes now indiscernible
in molded earth
no phoenix bird
has flown forth…
or maybe it's
he.
and me.
we fiery winged
brothers fly
forth and back
and delight in seeing
something…
or humanity.
our humanity.
cleared fields once,
now slowly reclaimed
by persevering forests.
somehow comforted
by this:
peaceful persistence.
leaf-ambered stream
flows cold and steady
unrelenting renewal
and movement
just like everything else.
somehow comforted by this:
peaceful persistence

Snow Falls Down
Boulder, CO – 1997

Snow
    falls
        down
            slowly
                down
                    floating

I sit
    write
        logos-bound
            but discover
                share
                    humanity

We
    on threshold
        stand
            soon
                choose
                    ourselves

Some
    remain
        seated
            a few
                walk
                    all move
                        somehow

>>>

>   Movement
>   always
>   virtual, actual
>   swirl in
>   this cosmic
>   mosaic
>   this
>   convoluted
>   humanity
>
>   We forever
>   floating
>   wind
>   down
>   rest
>   melt

Strange the Marriage
Early Winter, Boulder, CO – 1997

Strange the marriage:
Logos, PNP
and my contempt for each;
for the former
is ticket
of modern nomad
until
we realize
The Return
to Be

---

* *PNP = "post nomadic phenomenon," ie: birth of "civilization" as we know it (agriculture, city-states, socio-political stratification, slavery, increasing ecologic destruction/desertification, writing, etc.).*

Sun Down Now
Early Winter, Boulder, CO – 1997

Sun down now
bright spot
on mountain silhouette

Liquid sky gold
flows upward
from dark peaked well

Jagg'd shadow slides east
golden sun flies west
penumbra augments

We zig zag shutter
dart and weave
relentless human doings

Walkers sit, watch
biped ant bustle
and wonder, just wonder.

This that yes no
system says so
most concede

I can't
oft' wish I could
even should… can't

Just wonder just wonder
feign ant hustle
time to time

Detatched, distanced
eyes open to goings on
I wonder   just wonder

From Modern Hands
Boulder, CO – 1997

from modern hands
beat tribal rhythms
machined messages proclaim
TIME IS OFF

laughter explodes from within
deep deep self abyss,
brahma, ubiquitous and
swirling hot jazz mosaic
explodes: Logos Vulcan lava laughter

so much energy
so much energy

on frozen concrete
I sit and think
visit familiar visions:
verdant, sun-filled happiness
I see some land, promised
but fleeting, promised
but vague, promised
but imagined, a dream…

dream is hope
dream is life energy
dream is poiesis song
and dream lined rhythm
    is reality
    a reality
    my reality
I wonder, hope dream
   view promised land

>>>

>   splendor and
>   walk
>   keep walkin'
>   wonderin'
>   hopin' that we
>   may someday
>   arrive
>   return
>   relearn to forget
>   TO BE

Gnarled Spruce Blues
Boulder, CO – 1997

gnarled spruce blues
enveloped in air
thin, pure
spirit

we wait slowly,
quickly, soon
lofty limbs
deep roots
become

blood-inked poesis:
aphoristic oases
float in mind
but remain
unspoken…

…for now…
quiet.

we quickly wait
laugh slowly
and listen
soft steps
bellow:
ubermensch.

last men
behind, howling:
slow fade
in distant
darkness

unmoved,
we move on
remember earth.
become earth.
be.

Mist Droplet
Boulder, CO – 1997

mist droplet dangling
from green leaf

Tired Branches
Little Falls, NY – 1997

tired branches
grow
   bend
      crack
fall below
unable to behold
green sprouts
peeking from behind
greyed bark

generations
upon generations
upon generations
ever evolving
something tree
humanity
that looms and
dances
o'er me

i weep laugh weep
a patient audience
in great expectation
of intermission
or denouement
or post-encore bow

>>>

and final exit
goodbye-vanish

relief, fulfillment…
lest we be immortal
thank God we're
a mortal creature
there's no other salvation
death is Christ
Amen.

death life
river smiles
to realize
absurd nothingisms
of trueness
somehow

We Gather
Boulder, CO – 1997

we gather
    meld
        smile
            roar
energy swirls
    creating
        energy
            swirls
                creating energy
                    swirls
                        creating
                            energy swirls…

…creating…

poiesis song
resounds
within
throughout
us

we've gathered
    to meld
        in becoming
            we slowly be
                slowly are
                    quickly now

and I watch
    smiles
        hugs
            laughters
            roars

    thick rushing cosmosea swirls among
                us
            within us
                us

We March Quietly
Boulder, CO – 1997

we march quietly
unranked
or mosey rather
singing great songs
discordant
or hum to ourselves, rather

no more czars
emperors
kings rulers
dictators – all
now gems on
humanity's dazzling necklace – history
it's called by some

but we're still oppressed
somehow,
or will be soon
by ourselves…
our minds
us.

elusive intellords
bind us to misery
unsmiling days
of travail, tired
we slumber each night
undreaming
some wonder

some briefly glimpse
morning sunshine
in unwalking movement
to other domus, another
aedifice
I cry.

endentured now,
to ourselves.

But some will
break free
get outside
and realize
experience
undying human spirit
that's so often
eulogized

free   free   free
we cry
and hope
and dream…
sometimes…
some of us.

ourselves, I say
we must free
ourselves
from ourselves

*I hold the most archaic values on earth ...
the fertility of the soul,
the magic of the animals,
the power-vision in solitude...
the love and ecstacy of the dance,
the common work of the tribe.*

—GARY SNYDER

We Soon Recrudesce
Boulder, CO – 1997

We soon recrudesce*
L'hommes nouveaux
Humanity

Springtime sproutings
From dark musty
Mould… burnt
All winter
By frigidity
And harsh rains

Grey fogs lift
Float elsewhere
Slowly
As we blink, no…
Squint
In rediscovered brilliance

* *Recrudesce: To break out, become active again*

We're From Kuchu Sharvi
Boulder, CO – 1997

we're from Kuchu Sharvi*
smiling
sunsplashing
        down
                day
                        waterfalls

sage raga
        warms
                mellows

soooooooooooooooothingly,
                    now ->
sort of.
forth and back
        slipping
                enveloped
                    beheld
cosmos mother
Gaia
Earth
from Kuchu Sharvi
we're
we are

                                            sort of.

* *Kuchu: To Be. Sharvi: Divine; Gender : Female; Numerology : 5*

Wretched
Boulder, CO – 1997

wretched, torn heart
pulses fiercely
in a world
without honor
without dignity
without integrity
without peace
maddened mind
cries out quietly
as trembling body
briskly walks
through frigid winter lands
that bring calm
fleeting peace
but real
and felt for awhile
I weep

Sunshine Gushing Up
Adirondack Mountains, 1997
Speculator, NY – Christmas/New Year's

Sunshine gushing up
from mirrored winter lake
bathing all in silent warmth

ice sheets cracking
spreading in negentropic
symphony of sounded rhythms

thick black waters
below flow, gurgle
whale songs from some
abyss source

unfathomable splendor
and slight breeze stirs
in happy affirmation

I, perched on frigid
boulder throne drink this in
head tossed back in
sentuous submission
tingling as heart body
is pierced, penetrated
by natural energy phalli
or, I'm in some elusive
ubiquitous womb
ever-changing chamber
of life
without walls without boundaries
happy infant, I sit
pleasured woman, I tremble
virile man, I calmly
make love with uber-woman
energy of great mistress earth

Some untwisted Oedipean amor

Here and it's so beautiful
C'est trés trés beau, l'amour de la terre

I sit still dancing and
birth myself anew in
peaceful overwhelming
procreative orgy
with Mother
Cosmos, ever-nothing
great great intercourse
of conceived world
eternal birthing of now
in sacred copulation

I tremble.

*A poet looks at the world
the way a man looks at a woman.*

—WALLACE STEVENS

Ecocapricitopic
Boulder, CO – 1997

capricious world, ours.
embrace it, some
tremble, others
weep still others
the crazy howl
and roar:
lion-laughter:
golden enlightenment
so aphopatia's the song.
poiesis-paradox paradigms
now sprouting seedlings
eager in dawn
dew drops dangling:
crystal green globes
of ocean
great sea: B - - - - -
splashing, we rivulets
squirm, slide fly
to setting sun sea
golden so golden

absurdity:
vivacious caprice
our world
growing strange change
fathomless
cosmos
negentropic
like ligeti's
human eulogies
which are whale songs
which are forest cycles
celeste movements ubiquitous
poiesis
ecocapricitopic

Biotopic Villages
Moab, UT – 1998, Winter

biotopic villages:
  sprout,
  grow,
  green.

brown ochre aqua
  crimson
  bird
  soar

ashes phoenix fire
  raging
  scorching
  fresh

cleanse . . . stream
  icy
  tepid
  placid
  flow

we drink
  walk on
    drink
      walk on

übermensch oasis
  gathered
  sing
  drum
  laugh

green blue green
  sprout
  grow
  green

Come Down Rivers
Nederland, CO – 1998 (est)

come down rivers
comb me
brush overv
my broken flesh
crazed mind
calmed soul
and soothe
cold water flowing
liquid ice
sharp
heavy air
slick, naked
I'm enveloped
consumed
drenched and
shiverquivering
smile freeze
laugh dark
breeze blows
and in mind
trees dance
sway shadows
skip hop blow
come down river
over flow

Brick Path
Location Pearl Street Boulder, CO – appx 2000

meticulous brick path
lies red
                frozen
                      angled
still to the sands
    the wheels the feet
      still to the stream
        still to the wind
over and over tread i
this cubed clay mosaic
brick path moves not

but today as i gaze
far into the misty fumes
and the horizon
                the space
red path swirls
slides along side feet
  and wheels
flows with stream waters
  brisk air flutters
and eyes become dizzy

still meticulous brick path
forever frozen   but
  forever flowing
    as far gazing i's
tread over and over

still meticulous path of brick
flows swirls melds
  with eyes

Cooperative Narcissism (At a Poetry Reading)
Denver, CO – 200x

solipsistic I's converge
on solemn night of laughter
assuming selves of existence...
cooperative Narcissism
and clap
  in between
    reflection
      of mindsperm
        thoughts written
          on leaflets
            of our god
we convene tonight
as before
  the gods did
    the same bowing
      with soar fingers
        and preserved
          forever on leaflet
            God... papyrus
scream whisper weep
into small phones to others
which we hardly know
to be gods, yet, not dead.
so now Allen's god
with others ->
  thrust up in the sanctified
    hall of poiesis
      singers now silenced
and we mistake
for gods
but they're gods as well
we hardly see... our
mirrors abound for us
each other gods as
still ponds and echoes
nearby hint of other
  gods... but we're
consumed in ourselves
forever embraced within
ourselves, feigning to share
with some
other poets to
reassure us that
we may be
but not seeing
that we are
spilling Logosperm
to the wind the
Spirit the Caelum
now dark ever
flowing twinkle
sphere... that
many take for
a mirror...
  to gaze
    in

In Durango Pub
Durango, CO – appx 2000

slow minstrel
black felt beret
caps long seen eyes
that weep and smile at once

from Paris or NY or Frisco
but sits now in Durango
four corner minuets
Mozart floats amid young
smiling great grandchildren
of cowboys from out east
somewhere

now here somehow
in pub over desert sand
and dusk's settled into night
already outside quiet
coyotes we've heard not
but so soothing the old school
jazz…   of sorts

Tranquil Night
Durango, CO – appx 2000

slight breeze in
blows steady
quiet

hushly lit dim
room of slumber

timber creek
sounds echo
slowly

feint grumble
hiss autos
pavement roads
hum back
forth

desert nearby
beckons
glimmering light
shimmering night
of mind
is calm
quiet

dreaming
eyes open
gold blue
moon sun
embracers
of manifest
or mani-
pulated
some divine
hands
ours
mould carve
shape

us
to return
to us
soon
forever
as always
and clay
vessels
of soul
drink
spirited
liquid air
in aquarian
vase or urn
or jug
to share
and spill
and soak
roam flow
soothe
cascade rest still
pond on
moonlight
twinkles
our eyes
to form
the minds
of us

drinking
cool desert
breezes
in through
golden room
of shadow
quiet
humming
tranquil
night

We Mist Children
Appx 2000? – Denver?

second mated
upright primates
we... walkers
lost now in
Babylon's thickness
darkness... cursed
in our lean season
city centers
self centers
so our tribe's
a cry on the wind
and we still
stuffing bellies
filling lungs
smoky air of
mindlessness
not necessarily
the mindful
mindlessness
of the ancient
silver eyed seers.

floundering in the
mess of our parents,
our parents' parents
we slide glide toil
through the muddy
civil muck and hope

return return return
the ancient
the sacred
the Way... Tao

reluctant we children
of many tongued Babyl
cities... forlorn
amid millions

lost and unguided
in the presence
of the sat guides
but few listen...
few see... few learn

quote not the ancients,
ye learned man...
live them... invigorate
with the old old school
letters Logos Animas
Lumen Lux lead to
Ahimsa and Brahmacharya

we mist children
soon return...
unbeknownst to many
to our mother womb
misted Gaia and
great spirit Ra
Jahweh Sol
where all spirits are one
Namaste and write
pure Logos on the Book
Akasha becomes
clean again in such
time time tick
not time but, swirl
of heaven animas or
spirits or animals
du Zodiac and we
Zoan Politica in old
Athenian or Cretan
or Yucatanian or
Iberian or Himalayan
extensions live
true

Mind Junkies Need Gaia Cure
Colorado? – 200x?

Mind
Crazy conqueror
Infests the world
Logos-colonies
Ever expanding
'Cross otherwise
Harmonious
Earth

We
Info-fix
Addicts, hooked
Beyond reckoning
Averted eyes
Turn to
Darkness

I
Dip ink
For oil hangover
Then paint, vain
Color search,
Rest eyes in
Key strikes
(Black/white).
But tire
Go outside
Walk

Gaia
Perfection
Everywhere green
Blue brown yellow
Song wind splendor
Consumes beholds
And in new
Freshness, life

We wander
Back inside
Art

Candle
Shadow casts
AS we huddle
Entertaining mind
Word, image, sound, thought
And we pale, decay
See no moon
Feel no wind
Dying slow
Numb

Mind
Info-fixed
Monarch sits
Atop shriveling corpse
Found best junk
And build more
Colonies, fast
We need
We need
More

Awake.
Set down
Intellect-syringe
And hasten to desert
Harsh, deadly, rough
Beauty of wind spirit
Perfection and cure
For we're sick
Must leave
Go

Oh World!
Colorado? – 200x?

oh, world!
just give me passage
cross your varied surface...
allow me to walk quietly
along your rainy night streets
give me freedom to hum and muse
to your winds... this crazed
ancient wizard from
distant grey lands of yore
forever walking
forever gazing with eyes blazing
and embracing your depths
with silvered sacred ears...

just give this old soul
fogged morning ambles
through green dripping forest
paths... and some occasional
walkers to share smile glows
some mountain valleys
   to get lost in...
some peaks and falls
   to find

oh sacred world give yourself to me
a humble servant
a devout initiate
a walker... quiet, invisible, present
oh, world, oh great world
let me be

I Must Just Listen
Colorado? – 200x?

loosing myself slowly
and haven't words to explain…
I'm loosing those, too

slipping slipping away, this world
my mind's imagings, expectations
wants of self floating away

blown off by life's winds:
my mind's namings, creations
of world… blown far away

and me with them…
floating, drifting afar…
out into some cosmic void

and here remains some other a----
walking, eating, laughing, hugging
wondering to where it's all going

but still living, still learning, still pathing
and in float words: Tao, the way
of resignation to a world of infinite turns

endless rocks over which this river stumbles
flowing on and on to some distant sea
growing ever close, ever huge

ever daunting and ever consoling
take me soon oh winds to this great
grey misted pond of infinite reflecting crystals

down down this watery path flow i
mists cast off in great winds
forever blowing across me

i must just listen
i must just listen
i must just listen

to the Hum…

Seven Fathers
Hummingbird Ranch, NM – 2001 (est)

Amid storms and grey mist
The Seven Fathers of the people of the moon
Migrated from the east.

Across the ocean of Atlantis
They sailed in small bands at first, later in droves
From the distant land Europa.

In ages long forgotten
People of the Stars and People of the Land had traversed our globe
Even before that People of the Sea traveled the great mythic oceans with ease.

But as the Seven Fathers of the Moon People came westward
They embarked on an even greater voyage than was known
They had set sail into the dawn of the fifth age.

Synchronistic Encounter
Nederland, CO – appx 2001

Synchronistic encounter
With soul-brother, Earth-traversin'
Şaunuk... and like whispered
Reminders from Morgenlandfahrt, the
Journey to green vibrancy persists
The multiplicitous caravan of
Purposed wanderers creates its
Caravanserai from waters of deep and
Ancient inspirations. And so I learn
How alive and how forever morphing
Our digital noosphere ... the web ... is
And is becoming. Roots, würzeln, and
The soul-trees of these twilight –
Connected familiars will burst into
The winds... collaborating to recreate
The Ur-wälder of unremembered pasts
And forever returning futures. Şaunuk
Great flame, vortex, nexus of poiesis
And his song is oh-so-inspiring, oh-
So delicious. I savor this encounter...
And take lessons from the greatest
University – the University of Now and Here...
Amice-teachers lead each-other to
The wellspring... all students, all masters
Go We Go   Be We Be   Love We Love

Behind Horizon
Hummingbird, NM – appx 2002 est

Walking from behind the horizon
Milking
        A pulsing
               Star with
                      My eyes
               I quiver quietly

An awakening of
Global Nerve Matrix
Not so much a digital/cybernetic web
Though this may be syndromic
But the new quickening of a biologic/energetic
Web of life and aroused consciousness

Healing Waters
CO? – appx 2002 est

Magic rides a heavy night air
First snow down, lightly
Wafting, feathering, caressing
Gently decisively embracing
Our entirety.

Mother song, womb song
Gurgles up through infinite
Caverns and dances through
Her children... Healing nodes
Are vitalized, activated.

Spiral flows further into
Itself, freeing itself from
Its own temporal impositions
Star seed wills to sow
Itself anew: eternal serpent
Coils, weaves life.

Touch, authentic, deep catalyst
To awaken our own corporeal
Dragon lines, kundalini flute
Opens to light-matrix pulse
Of engendered universe.

Touch, medicine inducing cells
And DNA to dance the great
Shivic cycles that flow
Endlessly, great network of
Activation, symbiosis, biosis.

An Evening of Big Medicine
Nederland, CO – appx 2004 (est)

Ecstatic moans
Of pleasure
Triangulated
In steam
Cool tears
Rain true love
And devotion
The affirmation
Of shared and
Consensual betrayal
Beyond the bounds
Of normalcy
The fecund fields
Delight in our bare footed
Wanderings
Unexpected encounters
Are nutrition of deep growth
Temporarily broken hearts
Heal into wholeness
And we taste sweet drops
Of eternal embraces
On each other's slippery skin.
Hold each other in the moon's
Quiet hour

Poetic Winds Gathering
Boulder, CO – appx 2004 (est)

The poetic winds of my spirit
Nearly sufficient in exposure to
The intense heat and flames
Of rigorous academic learning
Now gather and spiral at ever
Increasing intensities
And will soon blow anew
Incredibly charged and imbued
With a focus and impeccability
Of the great forge's refinement
I hear the cooling waters of
Youthful passion and yearning
All around my being
Penetrating to the core
Beckoning my winds to dance
Upon the realized dreamscapes
Of my youth and a thousand
Youths before it
I am home for I am my home
I have awakened in my deepest
Dreams and have found you
My love you my comrade
You my clan you my gods
All here dancing with me.

Poetry is when an emotion has found its thought and its thought has found words.

—ROBERT FROST

Wet Moon
Boulder, CO – 2010

Springtime...
        Earthday...
Happy " " Day
Wet moon hangs over
        Cloud cushion foothills
Looking west; drip-drip
        Remnants of Seattle-esque
Downpour soothes...
        Breath
        Thought
            Poof
Into now, which is here...

        NOW

Et nunc, like the water
        And my daughter – she blossoms
And son waxes[*], expands, discovers
And the moon hangs heavy, wet...
Variant progrettiant companion waits,
        Bekons, hums that being song
Softly   Luminous Whale Being
        Of the sky traversing eternal
Modulation of woman, cycle, mood.

---

* *In the original version, I had written "And my daughter – she waxes/And son blossoms," but, for obvious reasons of aesthetic and poetic improvement, I have switched blossoms and waxes to correspond to the female and male, respectively*

Fire Keeper
For Indigo Hunter from His Father
(On Occasion of His 13th Birthday & Rite of Passage)
Boulder, CO – 2015

You are a keeper of the fire
This fire glows in your heart
As strong as the golden-maned Lion

You are a keeper of the warmth, the hearth
A defender of the home, the sanctuary
Sustainer, life-giver, transformer

Your fire transforms the elements
From wood to wind, from solid to liquid
You are an alchemist of love and strength

Your warm flames light the Indigo night with calm
Fire sending sparks of knowing up to the Heavens
Where star-fires twinkle in Eternal Creation Dance

You are tender like the fire-spark in the tinder
You are powerful like the roaring blaze with white center
You are loved and cherished as warmth and sustainer of life

Your family feels a warm love for your heart, your being
Your father feels an awesome pride for who you are,
An awesome pride for who you are becoming

The fire changes, and changes those around it
This is your gift, your responsibility, your duty
To stay grounded, heart-centered, calm in your strength and
    knowing

You now become Man, you join the club of big hairy beasts
Be a warrior, a lover, a protector of those not as strong
Be a force of warmth, of comfort, of safety, of sanctuary, of home

You have and will always have my unending, overflowing love
You are a keeper of the fire, Hunter
You are a son of the Earth and of God – you never walk alone

Soft Kiss of Winter
Boulder, CO – Feb 2015

As you look upon this heartfelt page
Be not afraid: but words are they
Now written down by my hand and mind
No harm can come as you read…
So please relax and be at ease.

There's a man now before you, calm.
Once a boy filled with yearning tumult
Unrelenting questions and questing
That gave way slowly to time and toil
To fatherhood and unceasing love
To cultivation and healing and growth
A desire for a whole, peaceful
Calm and joyful now.

A sharp and misshapen rock
Tumbled over and again by
The rivers of a loving time
Slowly, surely smoothed and polished.
Raging storms of becoming and painful
    searching
Are now a calm, warm breeze
And smile and laugh and love and care.
The forest mound is moist
With fading memory of a tempest.

And I see your eyes moistened too
By a deep water of knowing
A seeping flow of feeling
That cannot perhaps be held back.

Your eyes with a deep Moldavite green.

You, a precious heart-Shakra gem
Forged in the cosmic storm of life
Gleaming, beautiful, powerful
Both of the Earth and Otherworldly.

Before you through your moist hazel eyes
See a man no longer searching
For the thought of a woman
The abstraction of some nameless,
    formless ideal
That lived in the woody shadows of my
    mind.
No, I am looking no further
For I have found you, Winter
And will be patient with an unfolding love
Flowing together with you in a river of
    time
That cannot be rushed or foretold.

With you I feel a completeness
A divine calm presence
That silently assures everything is ok
But I also know that feeling and loving
    are dangerous
In that they can lead to pain
And my feel/think/act
And your think/act/feel
May only dance together as long
As we both wish and desire
But no longer than that

I know that a deep pain could follow
Should you choose to leave our dance
    first
But today I take that risk and
Yearn to feel again your soft kiss.

Ad Lucem – A Degree of Initiation
Boulder, CO – May 2, 2016

Last night in the dark room of reflection…

… a stream of memories…

THE THIRD EYE AWAKENED:

Blue Dog in the forest
The little people by the sea
Thus sun streaming in the desert
The ring-clouds setting in circle springs
Love-making in Valley View with W-----
And under the sun in the Cabo water
The sun dance and melting glaciers
And Earth's Mons Venus everywhere
Chanupa at Regis with Father Knapp
The spirit at Kairos hovering above, with two owls
Crossing above from their pine perches
The births of Osha and Hunter
Storm with N----- at Red Rocks keep
A----- in the Cottonwoods, playful
Lazy afternoons on Canyon with M-----
The "empty" stillness at the gray coast of Oregon

ALL THIS I REMEMBER

And cherish

And carry in my near-naked heart, as
Storm of B--- circles overhead.

Many doors will now slam closed.
Many more will swing open.

I AM NOT ALONE.

I HAVE NEVER BEEN ALONE.

So mote it be.

I Was Once There...
December 1, 2016 Boulder, CO

I was once there.
When it was all birdsong and wind whispers.
Waves of amber flowing in a great ocean plain beneath the peaks.
Endless herds charging all around.

And it was good.

I was once there.
When those ancestors came walking.
Stalking and celebrating the warming abundance with great gratitude.
Sunshine filling days of plenty.

It was also good.

I was once there.
When our forebears came charging.
Lusting that gold, those furs, timber, land, property, seductive opportunity.
Planting the cities we know today.

And it seemed good.

I was once there.
When women ran in horror and braves raged.
The taking of so much, even souls, it was almost absolute.
Tears and blood flowed together.

It broke hearts.

I was once there.
Great stonemasons carving and polishing.
Erecting monumental cornerstones and great halls to progress.
Justifying all with the great written law.

It overwhelmed.

I was once there.
When Chief Niwot in his Left Hand wisdom went east.

Adapting and learning the ways of the new white flood.
Preparing for the great synthesis to come.

It was courageous.

I was once there.
When they came with death in their eyes.
Shooting and slaughtering amidst the maelstrom of wailing people.
Our hearts were breaking.

It was heart wrenching.

I was once there.
When the lands were plowed and paved.
Endless hustling and bustling in gilded servitude to the great market gods.
Busy, so busy with it all.

It was...

...And then we paused.

I was there once...
When the whispering winds and birdsongs called us back again.
Slowing down, we began the great rush into our destiny of healing soils, healing souls.
We saw, and we knew once again...

...We are there now.

Milestones in the River of Time
For My Daughter, Osha Asa, High School Graduation
Boulder, CO – 2016

Marking a Milestone in time.
That daughter, now woman
Who rushed into my young life
Fresh and certain and determined
Like the River.

A stream, a conscious being, a…
A powerful Ursa-Bear-Healer
Washed over me and washed me
Down the River
Of Time and Love and Commitment.

And I committed to her
With my life, my heart, my mind
My sense of right and good, in…
In a confusing world in need of Healing.

And I committed and prayed
At the River, rushing
And held her up to the gods and
    goddesses
And the Queen Goddess our Mother,
    Earth
And our Father God, Abba, Papa.

And I became her papa,
Her one and only papa
And now she, a young lady
Crosses her own bridge into the
    unknown future,
That rushing River of Time and Love
    and Commitment.

And I hold her up, like before
Though this time not babe balanced on
    hand and arm,
But woman, held up by thoughts and
    prayers of love.
And I ask them…
I ask the gods and goddesses.
The River.
The Goddess Queen, our Mother Earth.
And our God King in Heaven
Our Father, Abba, Papa.

And I ask them…
Through tears of Joy and Sadness,
Tears of arriving at the end of this
    journey
Knowing it is but a beginning
Of many journeys to come.
And I cry and I cry.

And I cry out with thunderous,
Loving voice of Gratitude and Hope
Of utter Joy and Gratitude and Hope.
And I give thanks…
I give thanks for my daughter
She, that Bear that came to me
One night and challenged my virtue, my
    courage.

She that carries the Light and
Bears the ever-flowing Water Vessel of
    Life.

>>>

She that is with God and is of God
And is in Love with God and from God.

She that I held up in my arms in Love
And now hold up in my thoughts and
    prayers in Love.
She that now stands on the threshold
    between journeys
And laughs and looks with that glimmer.
She that has come to me and through me
And that carries the Banner of Heaven
    with her
Wherever she walks, humbly.

And so we're now marking a Milestone
    in Time.
That daughter, Divine, now woman
Who rushed into my young life,
Fresh and certain and determined
Like the River.

The River. The Bear. The Babe.
The Woman. The Healer.
Who rushed into my young life, and…
And now stands on the threshold
    between journeys.
In Love with God and from God.

And I cry with tears of Joy and Sadness
And call out with my soft, silent prayer
To the gods and goddesses,
To the River, rushing,
To the Goddess Queen, our Mother
    Earth,
And our God King in Heaven
Our Father, Abba, Papa.

Be with her. Be with her. Be with her.

Rafael's Song in Seattle's Waters
Puget Sound & Vancouver Island – 2016 – my 40th Birthday (October)

Grey mist hovers gently
Greeting ferries afloat on Pacific waters
Great whales of heart and mind-song
Swim, calling out our return.
Chimney smoke floats down
                Gently
                      Down...
Slowly swirling amid tall tree stands
Patiently, softly asking, assuring
After our hearts and mind spaces:
    Be calm...   Be at peace,
The nebulous smoke-clouds implore.

All around quietly dancing
Angel Rafael smiles and lights-up
Our wandering path with
Healing joy, calm purpose: returning and
    restoring.

We're back in the Ur-woods of our youth
The cathedral forests of our
Collective childhoods
When the moss soaking gentle rain
And cold crisp streams with running
    salmon
Sang endless knowing songs of
Abundance. And Plenty. And Wisdom.

And we too know these songs
Deep inside our beings, our cells
Know home and coming home

To the kingdom of emerald light,
Healing light that is the great
Green photon dance of life.

It is in the cathedral forests.
And it is inside us too.

Healing. Vivifying. Rejoicing. Celebrating.

Our (Great) Home-coming at last arrives
After long journeys, (Great) wanderings,
Pain, suffering, loss, and learning...
We now return to our Ur-home:
Soft Green Mother Bed
Of Soil Blankets and Moss Pillows
And Misty Sea-Cloud Sheets of Peace

Our arrival is not of middle-age
And slowing, but of a great return
To care-free-youth, only
Full... of care... and love...

And our joyful, laughing eyes
Are also full of deep wisdom-seas:
Penetrating, knowing, grateful.

Our quest of returning is drawing close.
Our quest of healing begins anew.

There Is A Center
Pristina, Kosovo – Summer 2016

There is a Center
Where we plant the seeds of ourselves
In the fertile Soil of our future.
And this center is our human connection,
Watered by Love
And filled with the Sunshine of the Lord.

We tend and keep this garden together,
And with the Breath of Divine Inspiration
Work humbly in the Soils of our World.
To help grow the Kingdom
And serve each other with Gratitude
And delight with Joy.

In the overflowing Abundance
Of our Lord's Divine Creation:
The Garden with a Center.
We plant and grow
Ourselves and our future
In this, His Sacred World.

★   ★   ★   ★   ★

June 2016, Fellowship Gathering, Kosovo

What If You Knew?
Boulder, CO – December 2016

What if you knew everything would be ok?
And you could sit by the fire in the depths of frigid winter
And think
And celebrate life quietly
And create

And it would all work out just fine?

What if you knew – what if you had faith enough in the Creative Divine
That you knew the flames burning in the hearth
Would always keep you warm and nourished
And would glow back at you the inspiration that lives inside

That is the seed-spark gift from Great Spirit.

What if you knew everything would be ok?

Poetry is the spontaneous overflow of powerful feelings: it takes its origin from emotions recollected in tranquility.

—WILLIAM WORDSWORTH

As Our Paths Diverge
For Winter
July 7, 2017
Boulder, CO

The world is burning
Aromatic smoky haze all around
And my heart weeps...
For you, for us, for all of us.

I will sing a thousand prayers
Of forgiveness, my sweet angel.
Never, ever would I want to hurt you.
But I have. And our sweet song
Is now bitter...

                                          ...sweet.

I weep a thousand tears
Dripping, flowing down to Earth
Like the glaciers in their
Rapid, silent, sorrowful retreat.

I shall not run, though.
I sit and walk and pray
I make soil and heal Earth
... and myself, with the Grace of God.

My heart breaks, and waits
For your return – perhaps in a week,
A month, a year, another lifetime.

I feel a glimmer of Joy and Hope

Know – praying – we will caress
And create the soils, ourselves,
Life... yet again.

As always. With God...

                                          ...I love you.

Grandpa Bear Passing
Victor and Little Falls, NY – April 2017

The deep, night, quiet lays in
Like heavy, cozy, clouds of spring rain…
And I feel you, sense you, in it…
Sleeping…

Grandpa, Grandma
Like the late nights when all others
    slumbered
And I danced and prayed in your cellar
    with
Paints and brushes and
The warm tingles of secreted wine.

I feel you inside my heart,
With me now more than before.
The way the old ones would sing about
In songs long forgotten by our people…
But songs that echo, faithfully sung,
    nonetheless.

They are in us.
They are <u>you</u> in us.
They are us now, too.

In that damp basement, I could smell
    and see
And sense our ancestors from the
    Old World
While you slumbered in bed above.
And now I sense you the same way
Floating on the wind, lingering in the
    fuzzy corners.

Watching, smiling, accompanying my
    thoughts and heart.

It is a sweet, disorienting, calming
    sensation…
The last of the Grandparents passing
Into the invisible mist-song of hereafter.
(Or, is it the there-before?)

?   ?   ?   ?   ?

Where are you now, Grandpa?
Aside our pulsing, yearning hearts?
Where have you gone… and how will
We <u>know</u> you there when we join you?

A beaming lad, eyes set on a grand hotel,
    astride
Some mystic mountain lake?

A terrified youngster – man barely – in the grips
Of war's living hell... that persisted in your deeps?
Or, will we know you as a pure lover, surrounded by the warm glowing light of Grandmother's embrace -

In sweet, unabashed, fearless delight?
On some great green, expansive fairway stretching before a deep blue sky overhead?
A peaceful, gentle birdsong-singing, squirrel-feeding
Grandfather who *sees through the veil...* and *speaks*?

How will we know you – how will *I* <u>know</u> you there when I join you?

All of those? Collapsed into none of those?
Miraculously expanded and refracted into your every-thing-ness by our Creator?

Or, are they lone sweet drops of <u>*you-I-we*</u> that we each remember and savor in fleeting moments of grateful reminiscing... by which we carry you – and ourselves – marching quietly, faithfully on into the eternity that awaits us ahead?

Trusting Divine Wind
Albany & Little Falls, NY – May 2017

What mean these blowings?

These gusts, these swirls, these blustery days?
I trust, yet do not understand,
Cannot fathom the nature nor intent nor tomorrow
Of Your Divine Wind.

I trust You, I trust Your Divine Wind.
Yet, I cannot know whence it leads me,
Whence it leads Us.
Your flow overcomes my soul, guiding it at Will.
And overwhelms my self, at times.

You are the gentle breeze that soothes, calms,
And comforts me – babe nuzzled at mother's bosom.
You are the fierce, roaring gale that bewilders, emboldens, encourages.
And you are the whipping wind that twists and turns,
Howls, erratic, and hurts… or so it can seem.

Through it All, Your Divine Wind is the unknowable Way.

Your ephemeral wind is always there.
Your weightless, invisible guiding hand is the grounded path,
More substantial, more real, more enduring
Than the sailing thought vessels of our minds.
More steady and ever-present than the varied weather of our hearts.

Your Divine Wind Is.

Is our quest to learn to Trust?

What are we to come to know?

Your Divine Wind blows us around and back in to You.

I Am Connected to Divine Feminine
Boulder, CO – July 2017

I am connected to the Divine Feminine
I am inside Her now,
Erect alchemist upright at Her altar
She pulses and I celebrate in gratitude.

Sometimes disconnected from an individual
Woman's Life-giving nectar;
That etheric substance – fountain of youth –
Flowing sweetly, from the well-spring of love…

     …the separation hurts.
Agony sets in,
Filling the heart and plexus
With a tightening pain.

But I am not alone, I am not disconnected
And the elder healer women
Soothe me and guide me
Back to Her – Divine Feminine.

To Her nectar, Her fount of life
That flows forth from springs,
Gushes from rivers and
Amasses in the ocean.

She is Home
And I am at Home in Her.

A Westward Quest – A Rite of Initiation
Aaron William & Indigo Hunter Journey Together... 2018

Together we embark on a westward journey,
Your morning sun of childhood,
Now rises into the noontime of manhood.
With the rite of the regular circle,
I pass to you the drawings, the symbols,
The words and chants of our people,
As we travel toward the setting sun together,
Slowly, patiently, unhurriedly.
In the timeless NOWNESS of our bond.

A rite of passage, right timing, right angles
Polished cubes hewn from rough rock
And circles upon circles upon circles of Initiation.
East, South, West, North.
Morning, Noon, Eventide, Midnight.
Youth, Manhood, Middle Age, Elder Years and Death.
It circles...
           ...always circles...

...And laughs and sings and dances and swirls...

So we travel into the mountain valleys, sit by the flowing rivers:
...from the Ancient Heart of the Mountains
And her hot healing waters, cool potent soils
....through the canyon land of sand and stars
Under the guiding light of Polestar and Planets,
Of our Strawberry Moon,
Full, in her silvery lusciousness.
...to the deep waves of La Pacifica.
And the towering giants with outspread evergreen arms.

To share the rush of the open road together.
To drop in to timeless, sacred sites.
To connect with land, soil, water, air and fire.
To connect with our Living Earth.
To laugh with Lion hearts.

>>>

To dance and soar with Eagle wings.
To talk and share the eternity of togetherness.
To meet all walks, and shoot hoops with the brothers.

To demarcate and celebrate,
To commemorate and share simple ceremonies
of GRATITUDE,
of MANHOOD,
of OUR LOVE.

Nature is not a place to visit. It is home.

—GARY SNYDER

Our Brothers & Sisters Gather
Boulder, CO – 2018, at the Star House

Our brothers and sisters gather
Laughing, praying, solemn and intent
In their rebirthing songs.

Mustard seeds, the smallest,
The Christos embodied everywhere
And our most blessed Virgin Mother,
In her watery blue ocean of love
Columbia, the Virgo dances,
Ushering in equinox balance

But don't miss understand Her blue waters!
Their deep stillness bursts with ripe fruits flowing
Our Mother – Her Great Cornucopia teams with a green life:
She births the pulsing multitudes of living soil
And Her Blue meets woman's crimson red,
She begets the violet, the transformation of Light
That grows all life within her watery womb
This great Gaian miracle we call home.

Violet – transformation – IS the unseen color
Of miraculous transubstantiation of Light
Into life – photosynthesis IS – it SHOWS –
It pulses, always, His constant stream of golden LOVE
That animates Her precious womb of
Infinite wonder. Life. Freedom. Will.

      You. Me. Us.

And upon our great altar to Freedom,
Our great mall of miraculous meaning and
Giant geometric gestures are pregnant –
Overflowing with an intention to bring balance,
To bring hope, to sprout with fertility,
To stand with the strength and justice of establishment

>>>

The great Boaz and Jachin are steady sentries
Astride Lincoln's forever pondering gaze.

What does he see?

We discretely sprinkle dew drops of hope
Into his eternally reflecting pool
Ripples reverberating with fraternal love
Bold Freedom rises beyond
The blazing sword of hope and promise
Marks the time with its lion-love shadow

A dial, a clockworks encoding the heavens above
And piercing, ever so gently,
        Humbly
            Reverently
The sacred OVUM, oval-womb-seed
That will flower.
And so we quietly and joyfully sprinkle
Dew-drops of hope at the juncture,
Enlivened by the Biodynamic forces
Prepared with love, horns, nettle, yarrow
Buffalo medicine and Lakota healing songs
The Sun Dancers' drumming songs
Under the blazing sun, weep and sing and
Shuffle the great dance of healing, atonement,
Flesh offering and transubstantiation
That is our work, our life,

Out of death: reverence
Out of desecration: joy
Out of fear: belonging
Out of the greed that grows from the sadness
And insecurity of disconnection from the Grandmother's:

A great invitation to rejoin, recover, restore, to rebirth ourselves anew
Under His Great Golden Gaze and Her Deep Ocean Eyes

So many are lost. So many disconnected. So many in an invisible
  amnesia masquerading as normalcy.

>>>

But WE know the Grandmothers.
We hear them
        And feel them
                And see their swirling toroidal flows welling up from Earth's own Merkabah

The great cube-sphere-tetrahedra swirling, spinning, radiating Merkabah
That is the Kaaba of Allah,
The Christ Savior's Blazing Heart
And Mother Mary's Deep Blue Well of Tear-Sea-Life
Compassion water animating all of this: countless INSPIRED beings swirl and glow
Merkabahs of countless numbers ARE the soil and forest and sea
And singing and dancing and laughing – for US as WE LEARN

To tend, to care, to keep
To steward this great Oikos-gift-Gaia-Miracle that is Home,
Our spaceship Earth
And WE are the myriad pilots and captains and servants to countless beings:
Numbers beyond the grains of sand, beyond all the mustard seeds – they ARE the mustard seeds!
That are in us – Her Life Pulses – in each one of us

Her Life, Her Christ, Her Mary

The Grandmothers are all here with us
And the Grandfathers are here too, gentle
In their warrior retirement and post-battle healing,
Soothing salve of the women's singing and smiles and embraces
Restore balance and knowing,

        Just as He and They all said – the Elohim – with Spirit hovering, watching, delighting:

IT IS GOOD!

And we need worry not about the WOE to we who heed not the command
        To keep and tend...
Let alone His command to LOVE!...

                                      >>>

We need not worry about those wayward, wayfaring souls – NO!

We set ourselves squarely to the craft and task at hand:
To cultivate Joy and Friendship and the Family-hood of Humanity,
The Caro and Kairos – knowing, LIVING THE TRUTH: that Logos is HERE,
    NOW with
Bios and Sophia and that
    We lovers of life and wisdom know, in gentle humility that we need

                  FEAR NOT!

For the greatest, the fiercest, all the power that ever was or will be is

                  HERE NOW!

And so we arrive, smiling, laughing, singing joyful and enthusiastic, nuzzled in the sweet embrace of

                  GLOWING LOVE.

Unresolved Stanzas (Incomplete)
Boulder, CO – 2018

In the great poem of your life,
Know some stanzas won't resolve.
They'll dangle, hang and sway –
Swings, forgotten on breeze of day.

Your life's a river, wide and great.
Countless stretches, bizarre and varied.
Each a breath, a moment, a chapter
To which you're married.

A river, a swing, a winding path
O'er the land, hill, dale and spring.
You walk, you rest, you sing, you weep,
You shout in rage, and dream in peaceful sleep.

It's all connected, all woven, flowing
And never ceases its constant knowing.
Who you truly are, from whence, to where –
It's yours and yours alone, as you wish, to share.

Who am I? – Weird Grace Flows All Around
Nederland, CO – August 5, 2018

How does a warrior monk
   Scholar
Healer
   Father
Writer
   Painter
Poet
   Accountant
Entrepreneur
   Leader
Speaker
   Consultant
Spy for the future
   Shin Rin Yoku – practicing
Teacher
   Brother to brothers
Child of nature
   Playful little boy in the woods
Passionate lover of woman
   Mystic
Navigate these strange times?

      …Weird GRACE flows all around…

To the Women I (Have) Love(ed)
Boulder, CO – July 2018

I have felt You…
All of you, at Once.
In the bright shower rays
Of lazy summer days.

I have looked for You
In a glass of Wine –
That glistening globe of
Sunshine-warmed dew drops.

I have found You
With that Wine in hand…
Laughing, embracing, riding
Those rolling waves of ecstasy together.

But then you left…
    Or tired of it…
        The wine…
Or me, the wine-drinker.

I now seek You
In a quieter stillness.
No Wine, no Moon-soaked nights
Of barely remembered Foggy Bliss

    No.

Just me.
    And the Sun
And Moon and Sea and Waves
And great green Trees…

And great, green Dreams…
…and that feeling of contented Joy
That was ours only in Childhood…
    Until now.

Dry, I am *always soaked* now by
The Dionysian Sun Shower…
And see You frequently in my Dreams,
Feel You eternally in my heated Heart,

Knowing this all exists in our Flowing Flowering Forever.

Shooting Stars Sailing at their Apogees
—or— The Cabin of Our Awakening
* Dedicated to Bob, Travis, Stefan and Nick, and their Wives and Children *
Steamboat Springs, CO
August 8, 2018

A shooting star sails overhead
    Brilliant, proud, determined
So purposeful in its knowing path

The sweet water creek flows forever
    Her waters coming down to allay us
Always ladling songs of serenity

That arched bridge of scrolls
    Tiny in its hobbit-path beckoning
Giant in its way of welcoming wanderers

    Like us

    Shooting stars sailing at our apogee

But back then, we wondered aloud,
    Could this silence, this tranquility
This beauty truly co-exist
    With the madness and bustle of the cities?

Of Denver? Seattle? Philly? New York even?

Oh yeah, Oh ye, oye hoots the patiently gazing barn owl.

    Oh yes.
Listen.
    It does.

The kaleidoscope of worlds,
    Divergent fractal crystals
Of thought and being and
    Experience all co-exist.

    Right Now.

>>>

Here and now, in fact,
   She says... and asks:
Can you expand your heart to hold it all?
   It hurts, it aches, it yearns... in our youth.
Oh acceptance, oh belonging,
   Oh joyful tribe of Dionysian adventure –
The bare-footed piano man,
The naked women climbing atop sun-warmed rocks.
Perched. Perky. Perfect in momentary memories
   That last a lifetime... if a bit hazy and dusty

Like the cabin of our youthful awakening.

Sits still, silent. Quiet in its contentment...
   of teaching so many unnoticed lessons.

Lusty nights of moon-song
   And whisky-soaked laughter
Bread-breaking and revelry complementing
   The solemn, serious mass and books and vocab lessons
In a collision of logos and pathos and Kairos
   Only we poets can truly see and feel
And taste

   And smell.

The waters of deep blessing
   The warm, soothing waters of hot springs
Our regular soaking sanctuary that was,
   In truth, a most precious, most foreign delight
To so, so many. Unknown to most.
   Unimaginable to masses of mankind.

This – this was our normal.
   This was our youth
Our becoming, our context
   Our hearth and our oikos.

This was the place of our awakening.

So we soaked in a Kairos of becoming,
   Eyes ablaze, hearts on fire and crackling,

>>>

Minds expanding and touching with myriad tendrils
   The great knowing-neuro-network of the heavens…
That penetrate and infuse all of this.

   You.   Me.

And the sweet, dusty memories that linger forever.

Back then we pursued and plucked the ripening fruits of young beauties,
Back then we lay alongside those sweet ladies' pale moon-lit flesh,
   Feasting on their sweet musty waters and young juice-filled flowers
Back then we soaked in a paradise while yearning for something else,
Some future, some other, some enticing whispers on the winds.

   Unknowing. Only awakening. Only making magic mushroom memories
   In the now-then-forge of foggy misty pasts that hinted at the Great One

But now, we sit still, smiling, as our little girls chase and pick berries
   Our little boys run in happy circles with sticks and swords and light sabers
Touched by the force that awakens us all –
   Some slowly, some in a flash, some in the steady,
Hot burn of a great shooting star,
   Determined in its radiance and direction…
Perfectly poised to flash great being-ness

   In a mere instant…

   …a moment that burns and lives on in the dark-sky memories of eternity.

So NOW we have to ask: we inquisitors,
   Trained and forged in the hallowed Ignatian halls,
We young bucks – cum fathers – we once lusty lads
   Now dads, steady in our fatigued promise to the next,
The progeny, the wave coming up from behind that
   Becomes our here and now…

We have to ask:

Does the flashing star know its halfway point?
   Does it say to friends and dear loves:

   Thank you.   Thank you.   Thank you for being HERE with me.

>>>

          For laughing, crying, expanding, hurting, learning,
          Becoming with me in that here and now of our-selve-ness.

Thank you.   Thank you.   Thank you
          For all those mad wine-soaked wildernesses of neo-epicurean exploration.

Thank you.   Thank you.   Thank you for being there…
          For sharing you, and listening to me sharing too.

While gazing up together at that shooting star blazing overhead
    Does it KNOW when it's at it's mid-point in the sky?

In the deep business of our fatherhood and grown-up-ness,
    Do we know we sit perfectly balanced upon the nadir-cum-apex of our lives?
Do we look in the changing faces in the mirror and ask,
    In all this supposed steadiness of me-ness, what changes do WE now WILL?

What songs, what stories, what poetry will we write NOW?
    For them, those sweet, brilliantly blazing children
Who will hunger for the memory, the echo of our souls,
    The details of our journeys…

    What will we leave them, really?

What of ourselves, our becoming will we share? Truly?
    Actually? Selflessly and honestly and unselfconsciously?

Not a resume or the prettiness we hoped to present our brides and lovers and women we
    helped make into mamas…
    No… not those polished stories!

The raw ones, unfiltered, unabashed
    The ones full and bursting with naked authenticity
With profound uncertainty coupled with curiosity and determination
    To do the very damn best that we can…
And   faltering,   faltering,   faltering

With the utmost sincerity
    That deep hot spring of love for our children
Fired by the star-flames of knowing:

                                                               >>>

We are ALL shooting stars in a FLASH,
                        ...AND...
ENDLESSLY FLOWING streams of sweet water.

And we need each other to mirror our humble human beauty that
   says again and again:

       Yes! THIS is Kairos, and GOD is everywhere – in you in me.
       In the children to be.

So let's ladle these sweet waters of memory –
   Awaken and rejoice for the first time in our
Knowing brotherhood of LOVE
   As we slowly learn that the children go through us...
Like Gibran wrote: They are the arrows, the shooting stars of the next,
   And we bows will find our comfort, our companionship, our solace
In the brotherhood and sisterhood of this
   Generational tribe of OUR OWN.
And burn towards our points of extinguishment together
   Knowing our heart-lights blaze forever.

       Together.

Poesis – A Man's Love of Writing
*** *This is the writing I love –OR – A Man's Love of Writing* ***
1/26/2019 – St. Julien, Boulder, CO

Oh dear gloaming,
Sweet, sweet afternoon
Of glowing rays and lazy clouds drifting: nonchalant,
Aloof and unperturbed by approaching dusk

You entice me.

You invite me.

Moaning, squirming like a young lover, ripe in her desire to capture, to behold,
  to engulf, to have.

And I smile, sweetly at you. With you.

      Delighting.

        And calm. Oh, so calm.

You have loosed your grip.
You no longer have your Dionysian hold on me.

    Not today.
No – instead of the sips of wine that caress, one by one,
Pulling me closer and closer to your songs and shores,

No – instead of swimming in the crystalline glistening of your
Sundrops kissing the golden waters of my chalice,

No – instead of enrapture and seduction and roaring, joy-filled ,
Overflowing – inebriation –surging with waves of desire and ecstasy,

I sit.

And write.

And smile.

Listening to the cello, the violin, the sitar…
Not to your drunken songs of allure and promise.

                                >>>

No, not today.

I will have you again one day, my love, my muse,
But for now I work. Calmly. Joyfully. Earnestly.

With devotion
        Devotion to you.
                And to our world.
                        And to what we can and must and shall

Create together.

I love you. I long for you.

And with patience, I await our bliss-ful, kiss-soaked, wine-and-nectar-gushing, joining,
Rocking on your waves, impervious to your jagged shores,
Sipping, drinking, gorging myself on the fruits and honey of your fountain,
        Your mountains.
                your eternal well-spring of youthful creativity and lovemaking…
And those thousand glistening pearls and diamonds of Hermon's dew atop your lips,
   your hips, your stepping stone spine, neck shoulders, nipples, calves, forehead, thighs.

I will have you again, my love.

But for now.

I write.

I work.

I worship steadily at Apollo's Temple, laying the bricks and stones, one by one,

Knowing, that I possess the breath, the flow - always.
        The Pulse.
               The Lost Word.
                      The Sacred Song.
                              The Sensual Dance.
                                      The Key of Dionysus.

To unlock the spreading bloom of your Bacchanalian temples once again.

I smile.

*Painting is silent poetry,
and poetry is painting that speaks.*

—PLUTARCH

New Stones Quarried
Boulder, CO – June 2019

New stones quarried, rough then hewn
Placed and fitted: our foundation
Solid body floor, squared and grounded reality
A place to do the work.

Craft-masters gather, bejeweled
And stationed in the temple of the Zodiac
I sit with watery dragon and her moon staff, vigilant
Brother Tyler stands guard without the door, armed

Protecting, protecting, protecting.
That soft, sacred inner sanctum.
Oh what does She cradle there?
To what mysterious spirals does she open Her book?

Precious sanctorum, holy womb
Celestial bodies roam and illuminate our Above
Two great pillars reach aloft
Beneath great caelum rests Her checkered floor

Our Earth Lodge and a blazing star at Her center

And a billion blazing stars in Her living soil
Waters flow… around lesser lights…
Each of the Brethren a vessel in our shared chamber
Reflecting, above, below; below, above

Infusing, transforming, transmuting.

Sophia and Christos work here, together
Quietly. Subtly. Knowing. And we ask:
"Who, then, sits at the North?"
Aha, smile the old white-haired Brothers.

>>>

You will come to know, you will discover them
When She decides to lower Her veil to you.
Patience, dear Brother, you must wait with Patience.
And learn your dearly charged virtues.

What charity? What Hope? What Faith?
To what Relief and What Truth do You Ascribe Yourself,
Tie Yourself? Around what pillars and what quests
Is your cable tow truly bound?

Do you understand the gravity of your solemn oath?
Do you feel the gravity of this sacred Home?
Do you hear and feel and see all those dancing about you,
And watching, intently, your every action?

Demeter, Hera, Columbia, Ceres, Liberty, Flora
Your silk robes flow and swirl like Her Great Spirit Waters
What Light streams and penetrates and enlivens you, now,
In this great Gaian neighborhood of Sol Brothers?

What great Merkabah stars do we stir and swirl in our Hearts,
Together in our Lodges?
What great love-lights do we spark and tend,
What blazing stars are ours to reveal to our world?

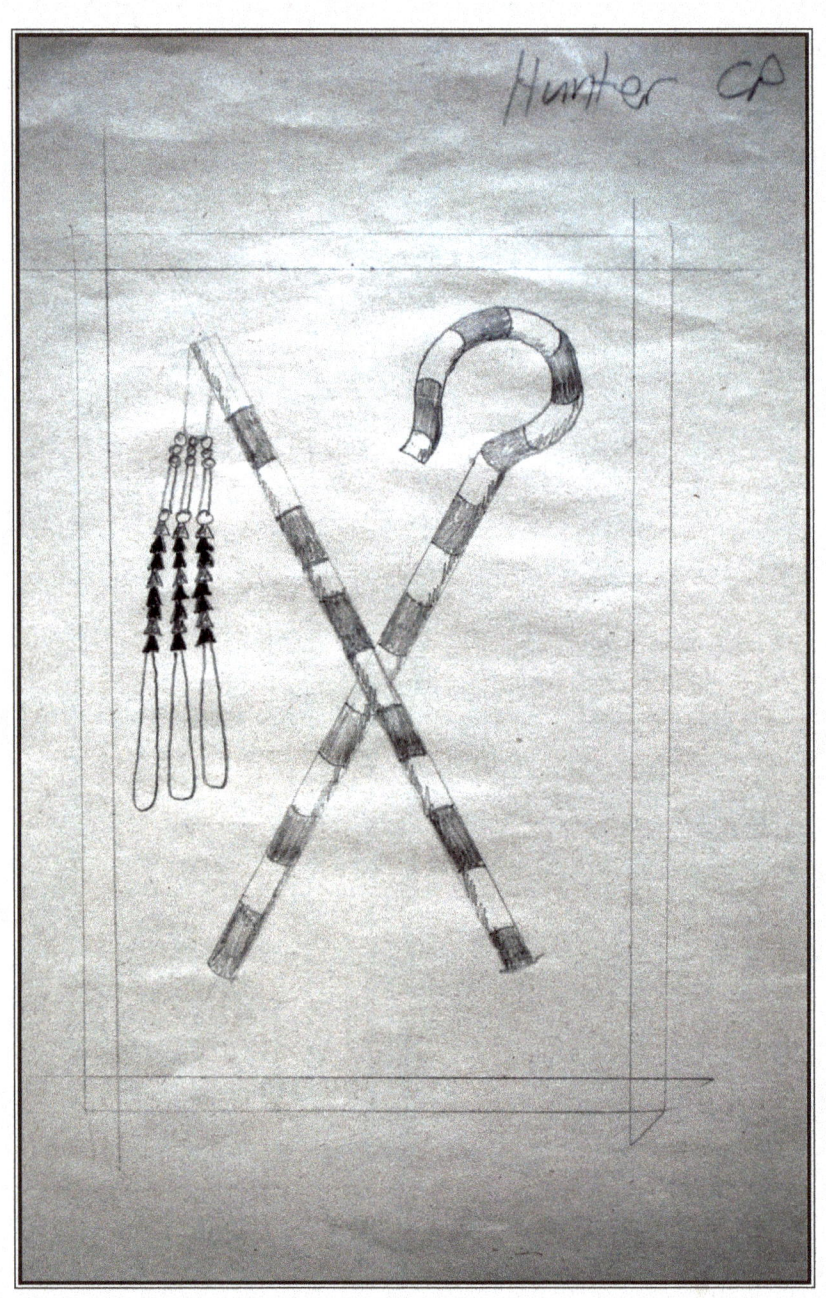

Wisdom Precipitating Into Our Bodies
Boulder, CO – Solstice & Holy Nights 2019

Wisdom precipitating into our bodies
Aether clouds, ordered, structured
In Cosmic crystals, creating corpus

Strong. Peaceful.

Our thoughts emerge
Vibrating into words of healing
Pillars: Demeter's abundant flow
The Virgin poised atop her capitol

Gloaming dew, honey exudes
Like Bacchanalian mana
Of sweet, learned luminescence
A watery inspiration, an Earthly prayer

Of song of dance of joyful ecstasy

And we delight in our labors
Begun in order, knowing from whence
The inspiration flows

A cross with three bejeweled directions
And a silent forth – the North –
The deep wisdom Abyss of Ancestral Songs

And Cosmic Light.

Oh dear child of the New Age:
What Wisdom, what Strength, What Beauty
Contrive YOU
       From this Formless void of Ur-Will?

What Piscean seeds do you plant
At this dusky hour;
       What Vessicas do YOU caress?
And protect, and revere, and adore?

>>>

While patiently awaiting
The dawning of the Water-Bearers

The Healers

The Caduceus Carrying Creatures
Winged, Grounded, Shimmering
In golden green

Veriditas

With rods and staves and flutes

Wrapped in Songs of winding serpents
Helical structures and sculptures
And odes to our own _____?
Child-like returns to Übergarten?

Initiated.

Adorning the World with New Creation
New Colors, New Hymns

New Wellsprings

Of vitality

New Knowledge

Novus WISDOM

A new harmony, watery, verdant
Emerges through peaceful wisdom
Of the ORDER

Our Order.

VERIDITAS.

We Are Creators
Boulder, CO – December 2019

We are creators
We seek beauty
   Each other
Ourselves.

We conspire with
   The mystery of
Hovering gentle winds.

We envision
   We pray
     We contrive
        We sculpt and sing

Our destiny songs
   Amid a choir of
     Smiling Angels

We strive
   We grow
     We leap
       We rest

And we celebrate
   Celebrate
     Celebrate

Our beingness
Collaborating with CREATOR.

Time – 'Tis Cliché to Ponder Your Vagaries
St. Louis, MO – January 3, 2020

Oh Time...

Tis cliché to ponder your vagaries
Ephemeral yet ever present
Swirling wind in the air
Rhythmic waves on the sea.

My boy – now man – grows strong
Yoked by the promise of vigor
The discipline of self-care
A misty mirror for father's gaze.

What is this... Time?

Do I sit atop a mountain, austere, peering
Into winding valleys of past and future?
Or do I descend into the cloud moistened pathways
Of ever-present serpentine now-ness?

Are you there with me, son?

In person?
In spirit?
In mind?
In heart?

In love?

My son walks forth now, stepping
Across an eternally ephemeral threshold:
Into a mysterious manhood
Full of familiarity... and frothing with ferver

I crossed that luminous line years ago.
Yesterday.
Always.
I cross it again and again and again.

>>>

And watch the crossing
From atop mountain peaks of perspective.

What is fate?
What is destiny?
What is family?
What is this... this aching love... that I feel for you?

My son.
My boy.
My man.
My... my... my...

Love.

Tis a choice amidst the misty ephemera
Tis a place to rest, to be, to know

Love.

Alesia   Алеся
(Boulder, CO – Jan. 28, 2020, her birthday)

You, Alesia, must be born
Of that Fierce Feathered Fire
Guarding the gates of Sacred Temples
       That you tend,
              You cultivate,
                     You energize,
                           You enliven.

You *are* the Temple.

Inside you are oceans and atmospheres of deep knowing, of love…

    Real Love.

And when you envelop me
In that sweetest Embrace of Shakti
I am transported
Into your Waters, into timeless,
Everlasting Elysian Fields of our Ur-roots
And into Cosmic Kaleidoscopes of

    Light…   … Now.

Fractaled, glimmering, a million
Crystals of every hue, surrounding

    Us both

In your embrace
And your eyes… Your Eyes:

    How do they ask and tell at the same time?

And your undulating Waves of Fluid Freedom!

    You are an Ocean.

                                                                                  >>>

I ask the Cosmos – are you to become *my ocean*?

    My temple?

My muse?   My friend?   My love?   My companion?

They tell me:
You are the one in my prayers,
Those dreams, those intuitions of my tribe
Those yearnings and knowings of
What's truly possible
With due patience.

Through you I feel Her waves
I feel Gaia's Green Gushing of Love
Ever locked in Ecstatic Dance,
Swirling Cymatic Synergies of
Embrace with Luna and Venus
Vibrating around Her mighty Sol, Ra – a Pillar of Strength

        And Softness
                And Healing Touch
                     And Gratitude
                         And Joy
                             And Fierce Vitality of Ever-Burning Love

Pouring and pouring out like
Sacred Golden Oil, Holy Honey – Welling up
In you, a Priestess of the Melissae:
The Kundalini Serpants and Happy Honeybees are singing and buzzing
Entwined and infusing your every cell
As your wild waves splash and crash atop

    My Pillared shores.

I smile. I wake. I feel you, Healing Goddess.

My eyes open to yours...

    The Green Golden Healing Light Swirls

                                                  ... I see You.

Honey & Two Red Roses at the Pillared Gate
Boulder, CO – Full Moon March 2020 – saying goodbye to Alesia – COVID Collection

You flowed like Honey
Into my mouth
Into my heart
Into my being

And I released you
To the sunlight
A faithful bee,
Gentle, honest, severe

               Tender

You are now deep, deep
   Deep in the living soil
Roots pushing strong
Into the dark depths

Releasing pain
   Harvesting joy

               Freedom

Mycelial networks
Light up for endless miles
Singing your Gold song
Your Light your Love
Throughout the entire World

I tremble
I weep
I smile

               Knowing

I have passed this most
Serious test of Our Lady

>>>

I have shown my
Courage, my valor, my virtue

She is pleased, smiling
   As Honey flows all around
I am now always with you

        Liebling

Two red roses at the pillared gate
Our hearts are connected
With the pure gold-green
Light of Veriditas

       I see you Liebling

She is with us, holding
Us tenderly, strongly, severely

He shines always into us both

       I see you

Do You Feel It?
Boulder, CO – April 2020 – COVID Collection

Do you feel it?
Do you feel the cosmic love of creation
Pouring into you from all seven directions?
Do you feel your sacredness?
Your childlike innocence?
Can you shed the pain?
Can you shed what holds you, stuck, in despair?
Can you let go of the walls you've built around your soul –
The "certainty" that suffocates and inadvertently kills you?
Can you break free and fly and love and grow and
Take good care of this holy place?
Can you become childlike in your humaneness?
Whole? Curious? Gentle? Kind?
Do you feel… **yourself**… longing to awaken and join you here
And now,
With tears and smiles and a whispered kiss of comfort?
Do you feel it?

1000 Dreams Forever (For Nicolette)
Boulder, CO – 2020 – COVID Collection

You walked in to the field
Dark springy locks flirting from afar
       … even then…

You flashed me that smile, that sign
And so I held one up:
       …"will you…?"

A thumbs up

Many moons later
We fly through Glenwood canyon
Seeking something new… fresh
And find each other
       …in Love…

Late night evening chat with red brick
Carbondale slumbers as we learn each other
       …entangled…

That night an invitation to join you
In your bed, as it rains.
       …a kiss…

"Never say never," indeed

Twenty six months of joy and bliss
And rage and tears
       …or was it twenty nine?

You held me to your soft silky skin
You kissed me wanting more and more
You brought me to your shores and
Set me loose, sailing across your many
       …waves…

>>>

Enya's ephemeral arias
And Guinevere's Green Eyes
Floated around us, surrounding us like the
      ...mist...

We smoked in foggy Maine forests
We guzzled coffee in deep
Bohemian nights of poetry and
Dark Scorpio broodings.

And then New York.
Young Scorpios.
      ...forever...

So now you only live with me in 1,000 dreams,
Deep, delightful, destined, hitched
In some other cosmic way
      ...forever...

Where Are You Hiding?
Boulder, CO – April 2020 – COVID Collection

Where are you hiding

        my Love,

                my Muse,

                        my Mate?

I long for you… why must I wait?

Are you the reward, to come, only after all the work is through?
        Have I healed and learned and grown enough to really see you?
            Have *you* healed enough, yet, to see me too?

I have loved before   and   been crushed
  by slamming doors.
My heart has bloomed with silky petals   and   been torn by thorns and
  ripped out Aka cords.

Why this yearning? Why such pain?

Is it our destiny to cycle
Round and round again,
On that whirling wheel,
Like Siddhartha and Nietzsche said?

I long for you… I adore you…

But will I ever know you?

        Here, on this Earth, in this Life?
        A dear companion on this journey?

                This chapter?

                        And many more, thereafter?

Where *ARE* you hiding?

Stay together learn the flowers go light.

—GARY SNYDER

We'll All Be Dead Soon
Boulder, CO – April 2020 – COVID Collection

We'll all be dead... soon enough!!!
We'll all be dead... and gone –

A song, no longer sung...
Unless it lives, persists, in the trees and soil and bees and dolphin memoires...
And in the thoughts of the great grand children of
Our great grand children.

What will they remember... of you?
What are you leaving them?
I don't mean money or houses, wealth or fame.
Gee, no, these are all gone – G2, G3, G4 dust in the wind.
No, I mean precious gifts like safety and beauty;
Precious gifts like healthy epigenetics and clear blue water...

Pristine neurobiochemistry. Pristine planet Earth.
They are one and the same, after all...

Don't you see?

Death will come for us:
You... and... me...
We'll all be... dead soon.

What will you do with this precious gift today, NOW?
What songs will you sing? What healing, what yea-saying?
What celebratory ceremonies will you lead?

WHAT WILL YOU DO WITH THE TIME YOU HAVE, THEN?

What, then, will you do?

    NOW?

Before you're dead?

What If...
Winter Solstice 2019 & Spring 2020 – COVID Collection

What if...

Humanity is on the brink of a great awakening?

What if there is a PAUSE...

    ...and...

What if awesome, humble healing powers

    get activated

        among thousands of us,

            tens of thousands,

                hundreds of thousands?

What if the great Veriditas

        – the Healing Green biophotonic light –

gets generated and transmitted across millions of nodes worldwide?

What if Raphael and thousands of Angels are here, now, to help us heal?

Will you feel it?

Will you see it?

Will you be it?

What if...

Do I contradict myself?
Very well then, I contradict myself,
(I am large, I contain multitudes).

—WALT WHITMAN, *Song of Myself*

Acknowledgements

As with any project of this nature, it was the combined efforts of several people who transformed scribbled poetry stashed here and there into this cohesive collection.

I am forever grateful to the Earth Water Press team for all of your input and feedback throughout the many steps and stages of the project—especially Moyra Stiles, Maya Strausberg, Jessica George, and Artem Nikulkov.

Especially deserving of my gratitude are Jake Welsh for his beautiful cover art, and Maggie McLaughlin who was the "wizard behind the curtain" pulling all of this together into a beautifully designed, artfully laid out, and aesthetically delightful creation.

I would also like to give a special thanks to Bruce and Marci (my mother) for sharing your beautiful writer's retreat in the woods so generously with me during these strange COVID months.

Finally, I cannot find words potent and laden enough with meaning to express here my profound gratitude for my son Hunter, and for the opportunity to collaborate together on this project. It began as a gesture to acknowledge and celebrate his high school graduation. It has, I believe, become a treasure that many more will enjoy and cherish in the years to come.

A Note on the Locations

Not only is this collection of poetry a celebration of special people and experiences in my adult life thus far, it also celebrates and pays homage to the places—geographic locations—that have been most significant in my journey. Some of these places I haven't seen in decades (other than in my mind's eye, where they remain alive and vivid with import). Others I continue to visit on a regular basis. These are sanctuaries, refuges, and, in some cases, among the largest and most powerful cities on the planet. I was born and spent the preponderance of my early childhood in the Pacific Northwest—Seattle, the Olympic Peninsula, and many Puget Sound Islands such as Bainbridge. Here I first fell in love with towering trees, soft moss, and glistening dew drops hanging from wise cedars.

I did most of the rest of my growing up in the Rocky Mountain West—Colorado has been home for decades. Not only do I feel an ongoing and profound connection to many special valleys, trails, waterfalls and regions in these mountains, I also have a detailed mental map of how they all relate to one another. Watersheds connected and interconnected by streams, mountain passes, hiking trails, and, yes, paved roads. In these mountains are my favorite hot springs, biodynamic farms, and generous stashes of high altitude medicinal herbs. It is in this setting that my children did most of their growing up as well, and so we share deep, meaningful memories situated in this beloved landscape.

West of here is the intensely forlorn and sun-parched desert landscape of the canyon country, the same such landscape as celebrated by Edward Abbey, Ansel Adams, and so many others. I have experienced things in these dusty, star-soaked temples that would likely seem implausible to many. Those are special memories I hold dear in my heart, and share with only my closest friends and family. Strangely, I wrote most about the desert landscape while backpacking through Europe in my late teenage years with Amanda, the mother of my children Osha and Hunter. We traversed from Ireland, Wales,

Scotland, and England to France, Germany, Austria, and Italy. Some of our most precious memories include walking the streets of Paris, drinking wine on a pillar of Florence's Ponte Santa Trinita (a laughter-soaked reprieve from some running tiff of ours) overlooking the famed Ponte Vecchio, hiking and camping in the Austrian Alps, and living on an idyllic family farm on the island of Corsica for nearly a month.

Later in life, my professional travel would take me to Slovenia and the Balkan region, and to landscapes of my heritage going back at least to the eighth century in the Kamnik-Savinja Alps. In upstate New York, where my parents and grandparents all grew up, a confluence of German, Slovenian, English, and Celtic peoples flowed in to the territory of the Mohawk peoples—the "Keepers of the Eastern Gate" for the great Iroquois Nation whose civic innovations informed the Constitution of the United States. My father's mother's mother was full-blooded Mohawk, causing me to cherish even more deeply the decades of memories in the Mohawk Valley, the Adirondack Mountains, and elsewhere throughout that abundant region—including Manhattan Island in the City of New York, where I spent the first phase of my college career. I have heard the name "Manhattan" translates to "land of intoxication," and I have some understanding of why this might be true. Those were tumultuous years, to say the least, and I now savor visiting that concrete jungle for short spells, appreciating the relative stability that I now feel inside. There is something about living for weeks on end in an intense vertical urban landscape like New York City that hurts me. I feel disconnected from the trees, the rivers, the birds, and perhaps most intensely the soil and sky.

As I wrote in the first chapter of my non-fiction tome, *Y on Earth: Get Smarter, Feel Better, Heal the Planet*, our connection with "Place" is essential for our health, well-being, and for the psycho-spiritual framework, foundation, and fabric requisite for us as humans to take good care—to steward—the living landscapes of this sacred, precious Planet Earth. Many traditions understand this special role—stewardship—to be the unique ecological function of our peculiar species, one endowed with capacity to work with the quintessence of life force to help amplify the creative, living impulse that is our Great Mother's generative essence. Without this connection, this relationship, we are like ships unmoored and adrift without sail or rudder, and we become dangerous toward the very biosphere—Gaia herself—whose generosity and abundance gives us the precious gift of life in the first place. I am and remain deeply in love with Place—with so many places on this exquisite living planet.

My prayer is that you, too, cultivate this depth of love, understanding, and sacred stewardship. I promise you will discover secrets and encounter experiences that will take your breath away. And, who knows, perhaps your pen will also flow with a poem of recognition, relationship and gratitude, from time to time.

Yours in celebration and gratitude,
Aaron William Perry
Boulder, Colorado – May 2020

About the Poet and the Artist
(Father & Son)

Indigo Hunter Chesnutt-Perry

Indigo Hunter Chesnutt-Perry is a 17 year old graduate from Clayton High School in St. Louis, Missouri. He was born and spent the majority of his childhood and early teenage years in his hometown of Boulder, Colorado. Art is among the activities that he loves to practice to keep himself in a creative mindset, and explore ways to expand his talents and imagination. He is a young man of many passions including: basketball, weightlifting, drawing, film making, spending time with his friends and family, and immersing himself in the beauty of nature. Hunter plans to attend The University of Colorado – Boulder in the fall of 2020 to study architecture and environmental design while working as a personal trainer in hopes of cultivating his creativity while finding ways he can help other people and the planet.

Aaron William Perry

Aaron William Perry is an author, social entrepreneur, consultant, mentor, and father. He is the founder of the Y on Earth Community, an educational non-profit organization dedicated to soil regeneration, climate action, community resilience, and culture of kindness. In addition to poetry, Aaron pens both fiction and non-fiction works, and is amazed at the power of the written and spoken word to convey myriad concepts and emotions, and to inspire the transformation of consciousness and culture. When he's not writing, Aaron can be found painting, hiking, hot-springing, traveling, visiting friends' biodynamic and permaculture farms, marveling at the gloaming, seeking out a soft patch of moss, and listening to the sweet and surreal messages of birdsong.

Earth Water Press

Earth Water Press is a boutique publishing and media company *amplifying voices for the world*. We collaborate with authors and thought leaders to help bring greater understanding, healing, and beauty into our world. Earth Water Press is a social enterprise, meaning that profits from its publishing services support non-profits including the Y on Earth Community, which cultivates soil regeneration, climate action, neighborhood resilience, and a culture of kindness through innovative resources and community mobilization. Learn more about this ecosystem of organizations at earthwaterpress.com and yonearth.org.

fin

www.ingramcontent.com/pod-product-compliance
Lightning Source LLC
Chambersburg PA
CBHW042025100526
44587CB00029B/4296